Flowers from Andrea

Flowers from Andrea

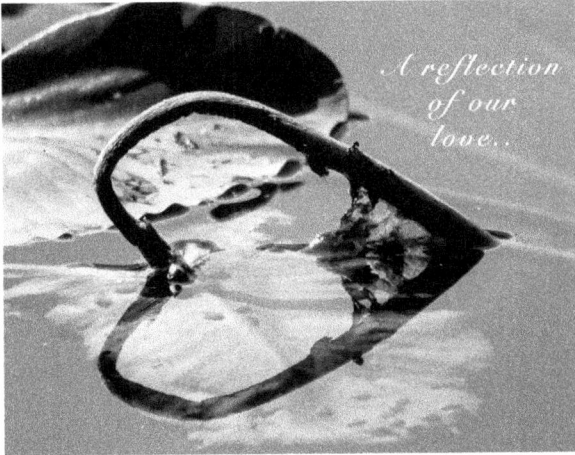

A reflection of our love...

A Grief Journey...and a Love Story

Dr Howard J and Andrea Adaire Fischer

Dedication

Dedicated to Andi, my wife and my love,
for always being here to walk with me,
holding hands, spirits entwined, as we travel together,
onward towards the light...forever.

Everything in this book is in your honor
and our shared love and creativity have made it so.

Table of Contents

Appreciations

andrea and howard fischer

To Carie Linville for giving of herself. For her time helping to facilitate in Greeley, for introducing me to the yoga studio, for being a friend and for her being willing to edit and critique the book so gently but excellently.

To Lori Klein for her counseling and support during my grief journey and for being my mentor as I learned to be a facilitator and for sharing her affirming and insightful comments on the book.

To Tom Rossbach for his friendship, for facilitating in Greeley and for his comments in the book.

To Roni Gruppo, Alfred Westlake and Kathryn Sparks for their friendships and for their reading a draft of the book and their comments and editing that helped to make it better. To Alfred also for Facebook (I think).

To Ronna Wellman for suggesting I go to the Community Grief Center in Greeley and for facilitating in Greeley.

To Dr. Debby Baker, the founder of the Community Grief Center for seeing that I wanted to help and giving me the unbelievable opportunity to create a support group for bereaved spouses and trusting me to do it with clarity.

To Tammy Black for yoga, the sound bowls, and Reiki.

To Beth Bullard for sharing her knowledge of publishing.

To my daughter Colette Washington for all her support, help and encouragement, and for the CPR School.

To my Granddaughter Breana Washington for the portrait photo, for her story in the book and for my earring.

To "Momma" Evelyn Washington for a conversation that let me know that there are many places where there is minimal support available for our community of bereaved spouses and partners. That conversation started me on the path to learning how I might try to help bring hope and healing to those underserved people and places and eventually to the idea of writing this book.

To all the people in all the support and social groups who have shared their stories and taught me so much.

And alway to Andi...For everything!

Introduction

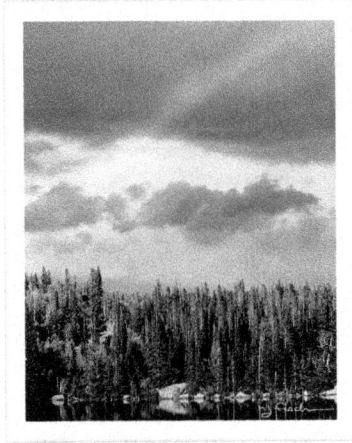

EVERYWHERE YOU LOOK,
THERE I WILL BE...

ANDREA ADAIRE FISCHER

BEAR LAKE, ROCKY MT. NATIONAL PARK, CO.
SILVERDREAMSTUDIO
LOVELAND, CO.
AUGUST, 2013

This is about love. It's not necessarily about loss. This is about a journey of grief and discovery and vision.

This is about learning and growing and filling empty spaces.

This is about spirit and living and rising out of the ashes of a shattered life into the light of hope, healing and wellness.

I want to share my grief journey here in the hopes that some of it will resonate for you and help you on your own journeys. That is my primary goal in writing this.

I know everyone grieves in their own way and in their own time, but I have seen that there are also commonalities and they seem to transcend our differences and allow us to help each other along the road.

It is also written in honor of my wife Andrea (Andi) and all we shared in our 32 year marriage and during the years of my grief journey that we have shared as well. It is also written in part by her, sharing her words and thoughts with me across the veil. (More about this later!)

My personal experience with bereavement is mostly from what happened to me after Andi's eight-year battle with stage-four Breast Cancer came to an end in 2016. Though I have directly experienced the passing of both of my parents and Andi's parents, as well as a sister-in-law, most of what I am basing this book on is what I've learned and experienced during the years since Andi's passing, from attending over 3 years of grief support-group meetings, and from listening and talking to other grief survivors during my grief journey and as the facilitator of support groups for bereaved spouses and partners.

I should probably start a few years before the story of my bereavement actually begins, and say that Andi's cancer journey changed our lives in almost every way. If it changed our love, it only made it stronger. As we traveled together through it all, I see us as becoming ever closer and our love beginning to take on an ever-growing spiritual character.

We began to be bound together not only by our lives together in the material world but our spirit-selves became more and more active and we became more and more aware of those parts of ourselves as our connection, spirit to spirit was strengthened and expanded as we lived through those times together.

I believe this profoundly affected the way we lived those years and the way in which we approached the end of Andi's time here as her body failed and she reached the end of her life in the material world. In many ways, it determined much of how my grief journey unfolded as well.

We had a magnet with a saying on it that was on our refrigerator for many years and it said simply, "There is no death, only a change of worlds." That became our model for belief and acceptance of what was and eventually did happen to us both.

Late in April of 2016 was when the change happened. It marks the transition of Andi's self to entirely spirit and the beginning of my bereavement. Although we had talked about so very many things during her illness and especially during the time when we knew that the end of this part of her existence was drawing near, one thing we never really talked about, mainly because we didn't know about it, was grief.

I had no idea of what was coming and wasn't ready in any way. When it crashed down upon me, I was totally unprepared for what it was going to be like. And I suppose, from talking to many others during their own grieving, that it is true for almost everyone the first time they experience the grief that accompanies the passing of a spouse or partner with whom they have shared a life and a love.

❀

So what I'm going to write about here is my grief journey. About the things experienced and the things learned along the way. In many ways, my grief was a life altering experience. The world as I knew it ended that day and over time, it contained an unwilling rebirth, a starting over, a phoenix moment in my life because all that I had lived for was changed forever at that point.

I am also a scientist, I was a Geology Professor. And so in addition to grieving, I also was driven by my nature to observe and even to document what I was experiencing. I have kept a number of journals throughout my life and I began a new one that day. I started writing every night before I went to sleep, recounting and remembering all I had experienced and learned that day. I ended up finding this to be not only a documentation, but also a very healing and helpful part of my grief journey so I kept at it and except for a day or two here and there, I wrote every night along the way.

This then is our journey as I remember it, as I wrote about it, as I experienced it, and what I learned from it. It contains many things and places that were very outside the normal way I experienced the world before the change. Over the years, I have come to "suspend my disbelief," to put my "scientist-brain" on hold and realize that the universe is much larger, stranger and much more complex and interesting than I ever knew or realized.

I've experienced things I intellectually knew about, had read about or had heard about but didn't really believe deep inside. I've had to change my world view to accommodate the new things I've seen and heard and experienced, things that don't fit nicely into the world as I knew it but that could not and cannot be denied in their reality.

The journey also contains many things I had to learn and relearn about myself and about living in the everyday world, about reordering my thinking and learning to make new relationships and finding new ways of spending my time. Learning to fill the empty spaces in my days and nights and learning to live with the loneliness and sadness and then finding ways to overcome them is a big part of what I did and what I want to share.

The journey also turned out to have a hidden gift within it. Because I had so much time, it also became a journey of re-evaluating everything in my life and a time to (reluctantly) recreate myself as I found my way through the grieving. I had to learn to slowly live again and "turn my grief into gold," so I could remember our life and our love outside the grief and sadness of having that part of who and what we were come to an end.

Here's some more about how I came to be able to write this book and where it's leading:

During the first three years or so of my grief journey, I attended a counsellor-led support group for bereaved spouses and partners called On Our Own at a local, hospice affiliated facility, Pathways for Grief and Loss in Fort Collins, Colorado. Many of the things I learned in that group have helped me not only in my healing but in what I am writing about in this book.

I want to acknowledge, thank and honor the Counselors (especially our lead facilitator, Lori Klein) and that entire wonderful organization for the special work they do and the tremendously positive impact they have on so many lives.

In addition to attending support group meetings, at the start of 2020 I began facilitating a peer-led support group in Greeley Colorado. Most recently I have begun to facilitate a series of discussion groups for people in the first year or two of their bereavement in Fort Collins and Loveland Colorado.

During that journey, we have also formed social groups that meet at local venues in town to let us visit in a more social environment that compliments the support groups many of us have attended or still attend. It has slowly helped each of us on our journeys to hope, healing and wellness as we are learning to live again and to become what I call "friends in grief." Along the way, I will share the stories of how these groups evolved and how you might perhaps join or initiate similar groups where you live.

Having now had the honor of facilitating grief support sessions and social groups for over three years in three very different communities, I've learned something about grief and perhaps about life in general that I'd like to share here.

Amongst the people I've met, there has been a wide range of backgrounds. The groups included women and men, people of different races, different cultures, different preferences, different levels of education, different economic backgrounds and circumstances; a pretty diverse group of people with seemingly not much in common.

But, the commonality that bound them all together was that in the end, they all grieved in much the same way. They all grieved because they loved. And grief didn't select who it effected or how it made them feel based on any of their differences or circumstances. Grief just hurt and they just grieved and when they were grieving, they really weren't very different at all.

❁

This is not a manual for grieving, it's mostly a series of stories about how it was for me and what I learned along the way. Since we all grieve in our own way and our own time, there will no doubt be things here that you agree with, that you need to know at that moment, and also things you don't agree with and don't necessarily want or need to know.

It's all ok. If you find things to take away from what I've written, that help you in your own grief journey, that is why it's here and why you found it. It's my goal to promote hope and healing and I share my journey in the hope that it will make your journey a little easier.

❁

The structure of the book:

The layout of this book is not necessarily linear. It's pretty open-ended so the chapters are mostly stand alone and don't have to be read in order. There are some concepts and ideas that show up multiple times throughout the book where I have expanded and opened up something and each time that happens, I've tried to fit them into the context of the discussion they are part of in their own way.

It's neither a novel nor a textbook, although it may read that way at times. It's mostly based on stories that illustrate topics and ideas to think about and see how they make you feel and so, again, you can read them in any order you want. If it's easier than reading it straight through, you can just look through the chapter headings and if you see something that seems like you need to hear it that day, go for it and see what you can learn.

Each chapter in the book is loosely based on topics that were the subjects of a support group meeting that we held in Greeley every month throughout 2020-22. The topics also sort of follow (again in a sometimes non-linear way) the journey my own grief took. They range from early grief that was mostly out of my control, through the early stages of healing and eventually to true healing and wellness.

I have put them in that rough order, again beginning with the earliest things I learned when I was just trying to survive, through the later stages of the journey when I was beginning to build a new life and then the movement from healing to wellness. But, wherever you are in your own journey when you find this, if you want to, you can just pick the chapters that seem to be about things you are experiencing or see what my journey was like through things you may already have experienced or have yet to find.

Since I didn't have any formal vocabulary about grief to use during my journey, I ended up making up my own terminology for the things I was experiencing and I've defined them the way I used them as they come up along the way.

I called the first part of the journey, which is in Chapters 1-6, Early Grief, a time when grief was in control and I was mostly along for the ride. The next and longest part of my journey, in Chapters 7-11, was about Learning to Live Again and Reconstruction, times when I was beginning to understand and take some control over what was happening and to actively starting to build my new life. In the most recent parts of my journey, in Chapters 12-14, that I've called Acceptance and Wellness, the topics are about reaching an accommodation with grief and all that caused it and creating and settling into a new life.

Between my own grief journey and listening to so many stories of other's grief journeys, I have also tried to find commonalities and lessons that compliment what I learned on my own (with help from Andi in spirit), to share the various parts of the journey with you, and share the ways I found to navigate them, learn from them and let healing grow in my life.

I have tried to write the chapters and stories in as close a way as I can to how and what I would say if it was just a few of us sitting down to talk and share our stories. I hope that will make it as accessible as possible and that you will find some resonance with the thoughts and ideas expressed here.

I have to remind you again that I was a College Professor, so sometimes I get a little pedantic and sometimes I can go on and on. I have tried to keep that in check and not be overwhelming in how and how much I write, but sometimes…

I have to say here too that I am not a grief counselor nor a medical professional. I'm just a bereaved spouse who has been extremely fortunate to have been given a chance to help others and in the process, to write down what I and others have learned in a way that I can share. I haven't read any books on grief and didn't and don't have any preconceived or really any philosophy about grief at all. This is just what I experienced and how I interpreted what happened to me.

It seems to me that there is a different perspective that comes from having experienced grief instead of studying it, and so, that is another part of why I want to tell and share my story and why it's written the way it is.

Feel free to use what you can and ignore what you can't use. You don't have to follow it or believe it all to make use of parts of it. It's just there to help if it feels right to you, and if it doesn't, that's alright too. Please take what you can and find what hope and healing it brings you as you read it.

In some ways this journey is fairly different from what most people experience or at least what they are willing to talk about. In other ways, it's a fairly common, and in parts universal, story of grief. See what you think!

In Hope and Healing,

Howard (and Andi) January, 2023

In Memoriam

I've written three memorials to Andi at different places along the way. The first was at and for her memorial and internment. The second was at the start of the fourth year of my bereavement when I launched a blog about bereavement. The third was at Christmas time, near the end of the fifth year of my bereavement, near the (seeming) end of my grief journey.

I include them here to honor Andi in this book dedicated to her in every way and because they are part of our story and of our love.

From Andi's Memorial (5/2/16):

I'm starting today with a very broken heart and I hope that what we do and say here today and the honor we give Andi will help me and all of you to heal and to go forward as better people for having known Andi in this life.

When my Father passed away, I said at his memorial that he was the strongest man I've ever known. I want to say here today that Andi was the strongest woman I've ever known.

All of you here, whether her beloved family or friends or members of the extraordinary team of medical professionals who helped us through this final journey, all of you contributed in your own way to us being fortunate enough to have had Andi stay with us in this world for as long as she did.

And for those who couldn't be here today, especially Andi's mom Vivian Radigan and her Aunt, Audrey Gladen, with their life-long love they too had a special place in Andi's heart and in forging the spirit and strength that allowed Andi to be the person that she was.

I need to thank Dr. Regina Brown who saw the path for Andi to walk at the very beginning of this journey and time after time reminded us that hope and quality of life were the keys to survival.

I want to add a special thanks to Robin and Pete Sewell, to Coreen, Ana, Kacey and Dale at Pathways for their loving and tender help in caring for Andi these last few weeks and for helping to hold me up and keep me fed, and to keep me strong enough to see this through. We couldn't have made it without you.

There was so much more to Andi's life than her cancer journey. So I want to talk a bit about it here because she was never willing to not be herself or do what she wanted to do no matter what else was happening in her life.

I want to start by saying that Andi taught me everything I know about strength and responsibility, and together we learned an awful lot about love and commitment.

Andi was very artistic. She had an eye for patterns and design that stretched into everything she did.

She designed the interiors of every home we lived in throughout our marriage and they were always beautiful. But of course, being Andi, she would always get another vision for how it could be, and lots of times I would come home and find that she had redecorated a room or two and wow, it was even nicer.

She painted, she did crafting, she was a natural musician at the piano and a published author of greeting cards and a writer of children's books and stories. I could, but won't, go on and on since these are just a few of the many accomplishments and talents of my wonderful wife.

All of us who knew Andi knew that at her core, she was always Andi, and her strength, her will, and most of all her grace through whatever came her way, throughout her life, will always be an inspiration and an example of a great spirit rising.

One of the things she always said to me as she so bravely fought the cancer in her body this past 11 years exemplifies just who and what she is in her heart. Andi always told me when it seemed too tough or painful or just too sad to bear, that there wasn't any point in complaining or feeling sorry for herself. She just needed to do what needed to be done in the best way she could.

No matter how she felt, she always got herself up, did her hair and makeup, got dressed in a nice outfit, and went out and gave the world her very best.

She always told me that looking and acting her best was an important gift to give to the people she loved and the people she dealt with each day. And with those thoughts, through it all, she always remained herself; she never let the battle she was fighting overtake her!

So today I want to especially honor an amazing, beautiful spirit and her great, compassionate heart and the truly wonderful and beautiful woman who was and is my beloved wife of 32 years (+7 more years and counting).

When those of us who were helping to care for and nurture Andi through the last stages of her life thought we knew what was going on, when we thought that she was getting too weak and we tried to ask her to stay in bed unless someone was there to help her, time and again she would sort of say ok and then quietly wait until we left the room.

And then suddenly, we'd hear a sound and go rushing back into the room only to find that Andi had gotten herself up, gotten herself out of bed, walked across the room and taken herself where she wanted to go. And then with that Irish twinkle in her eye, she would look at me and give me a little smile and let me help her back to bed.

Such an unbelievably strong woman!

She sent many of you in the family a photo this year with a quote on it that was from her heart and her spirit. Those words were pure Andi, clear and true when she said:

"You never know how strong you are until you have to be."

All of you who know Andi have your own stories of her strength and the grace with which she navigated her life and lately this cancer journey.

Many of you also know of the deep abiding love she had for her family and especially for her children and grandchildren. She was always a believer that it was better to give than receive and her fierce heart always wanted to shower her family with all the love and giving that she could.

So again, in honor of this woman of great strength, will, courage and beauty, I once more give her my never-ending love and know with no doubt that her spirit will be with me forever and that it will also fill the universe now that it is free of a body that was never big enough to contain it. In Andi's words, no more pain, rest softly.

A very special spirit has left her earthly body now and I wish for all who knew and loved her to feel the touch of her spirit as she reminds us that spirits are eternal… as is love.

I will love you forever my darling Andi.

Always and Forever!

For Andi at the start of year five of my Grief Journey:

I'm writing this a week or so before the 5th anniversary of your passing from living here with me to a wider place of peace, free of pain and sadness as your beautiful spirit was set free of the bounds of the material world.

I read what I wrote for your memorial, and after finding that it made me cry with both joy and sadness, I can't add too much to my feelings or to the expressions of love I made then and still feel today and every day.

Grief is such a complex place that encompasses so many parts of our life and so many emotions. It becomes such a powerful part of the lives of those left alone after a loved one moves on to their next adventure, and we remain, trying to create a new life and fill the un-fillable space they held in our lives.

Today is a day to honor and thank you again, as always, for the love you taught me and shared with me in life and for all we continue to be, to and for each other, in the past and in this new and unexplored journey we are traveling.

I learned this month, when I suddenly found myself once again crying in that deep, uncontrollable grief-mode I haven't felt or experienced in a long time, that I still miss our life together and the space you filled in my days and nights; with a sadness, loneliness and longing that was every bit as strong and all encompassing as it was in the early days of my grieving.

I have grown stronger, I am more now and have learned much, through your love and with your help, but I still miss you deeply. Though our spirits are connected, though we have found love across the veil, I wish you were still here, healthy and well, to hold and be held by.

As I do every day, I want to say I love you still.

Blessings on this day and every day and on another year of moments passed but always present.

All my love, Howard

I am writing this today on Christmas day, 2021. It's also five years and nine months since your passing day and it's the beginning of another new journey for us, a new lifetime of love, filling the spaces that my grief used to fill and celebrating love that would not be denied and of love overcoming grief and moving into a new way of sharing a journey across the veil and across the universe.

2021 was a year where my intent was to become aligned in body, mind and spirit as much as I could learn to be. As part of that intent, it saw the amazing feeling entering my awareness, beginning around the five year mark, that I was beginning to find the end of my grief. Close to the five and a half year day, I felt strongly that my grieving was actually over, that we had worked through it and that our love had come to fill again all the spaces and places in my heart that I thought were empty with your passing but that we have learned to fill in new ways across the veil.

You have now sent your love as (spiritual) flowers that grow as pink roses in my heart where my grief has been, and the heaviness and sadness have passed and been replaced with the roses and a smile that is growing to find its way to my face. And this week you showed me that my grief journey was indeed at an end, and we could now go forward and create another lifetime together, another lifetime of spirit, full of love instead of sadness and pain for either of us, and in the spaces that were now empty of grief and illness, love could grow again, and today you asked me to join you in that lifetime of love and to take another chance to let love grow between us, and all I could say was yes, yes, yes! Again, our love goes on forever!

Early Grief

Chapter 1

We are not our Grief, we are Grieving

NOBODY SAID IT WOULD BE EASY

WINTER ROBIN, LOVELAND, CO.

SILVERDREAMSTUDIO
LOVELAND, CO.
SEPTEMBER, 2013

thought I would start this chapter and the body of the book with two quotes about grief from Andi:

"Life is like a river but grief is like a flood".

"Grief is like waves breaking on a beach, overwhelming during a storm and changing to broader, lower swells that wash up less often and more gently on the shore when the storm is over".

Since this is the first chapter in the book, as I wrote in the introduction, I want to say that during my grief journey, I often used my own (often non-standard) words for thinking about, defining, and describing what was happening to me.

I also think it's good for me to include some dictionary definitions here at the start, as well as a brief description of what these words meant to me so we are all using these words in relatively the same way, at least in the context of this book.

Grief: is a deep sorrow, especially when caused by someone's death. It is a feeling within yourself in response to someone dying.

I think the important thing to remember here is that grief is a feeling or actually a large group of very intense feelings that come over you and kind of take you over. It is often totally visceral and emotional and not rational or thoughtful at all.

Mourning: is the expression of deep sorrow caused by someone's death. An external expression of your inner feelings (of grief) when someone dies.

Mourning is about your expression of how your grief makes you feel. There are many traditional mourning customs such as wearing sack cloth and ashes and keening, rocking back and forth and crying, and there can be many other things that your grieving makes your body do to try to relieve the very intense emotions and pain you are experiencing.

As with all parts of grief, they are your expressions and reflect who you are and how you loved.

Hope, Healing and Wellness:

Hope: A feeling of expectation and desire for a certain thing to happen. Grounds for believing that something good may happen. To want something to happen or be the case. To Intend if possible to do something.

Healing: The process of becoming sound or healthy again. To alleviate a person's distress or anguish. To correct or put right an undesirable situation. To restore a person to spiritual wellness.

Wellness: The state of being in good health, especially as an actively pursued goal.

In our grief journeys, what most of us are looking for and needing, especially early on, I found, is hope and healing. Our hope is perhaps that we will not feel this way forever, that it will eventually get better. It's not necessarily that we will be healed, however. I say this, although you might not agree at first; because healing implies an ongoing process, a change through time where an unwell aspect of our lives moves toward wellness. Healed implies a completion of the process.

An important thing I've seen and always try to remember, is that our grief journeys are always times of change. They aren't a destination; they are a movement towards a different state of being. We may or may not ever reach that end place, we may or may not ever be healed. But we can learn, we can grow, we can reach a new equilibrium and find a peaceful place to live within ourselves where we can find wellness. Do we ever fully heal? That's a "TBD" that we each have to first take the journey to find out.

So, what is healing in this sense.What are we trying to accomplish or move towards?

Based on my own grief journey and talking to other bereaved spouses and partners, I believe that what we are looking for is a place we can move towards and reach that allows us to hold the memories of our lives with our spouses or partners in a place that becomes less painful as time goes by, that honors them and the love and lives we shared with them.

I think healing includes finding an equilibrium between our past lives with our loved ones and our new life without them. I believe that when we are ready, healing includes surrender to- and acceptance of what has happened and what has changed in our lives.

As time goes by, we usually come to be more willing and able to surrender to our grief and accept the changes in our world. We start to live more in the present and dwell less on the past, we come to allow life to take over and grief to recede and we become more functional and comfortable in the new life we have been creating.

When we do this, it is us reaching a state of wellness that includes our bereavement, but where we are no longer controlled or debilitated by our grief, and grief has receded way into the background of our lives.

❀

A continuum of grief to wellness:

This is a way of looking at things that seems to tie a lot of what I've experienced and written about together.

When I was looking through what I had written about my early support group experiences, I realized that when I wrote about my grief journey, it was mostly about telling my story to other people in the group and living it in my head. When I wrote about my healing journey, it was about what I was learning from the other people in the group about things that they had learned and were talking about. Hearing their stories of things that they had done or experienced was giving me ideas that were helping me to heal as well.

Looking at it that way, I started to see that I was experiencing more than one journey at a time. While I've talked about my grief journey in parts of the book, I've also talked about my healing journey in others. I think initially I was using them synonymously, as if they were the same thing.

As I considered it later though, I realized that I had experienced and learned very different things in each of those parts of the overall journey of my bereavement. Although many of them were happening at the same time, it was more complex than that. Maybe it was more of a movement through time from one overlapping journey and what that one contained, to another.

And, of course, it didn't progress in a linear way either. As with most of my bereavement, there was a non-linear element to it. It contained a movement forward towards healing or wellness, or a regression towards more powerful grief, or sometimes a plateau where I was stationary for a time. And in addition, things changed in all of those directions a number of times during my overall journey towards wellness.

So this is how it appears to me after thinking about it for a while.

When we first become bereaved, our grief journeys begin. We start moving through our grief and during that time, for most of us, grief is pretty much in control. Much of the first part of this book is about that time, when we are almost entirely on our grief journey, experiencing many of the things that are included in the Early Grief chapters in the book.

At some point, that is different for each of us, we start to take control of our lives. We start to begin our healing journey. The two journeys, grief and healing; overlap. They occur simultaneously, but in the image of a continuum, our grief journey begins to decline as our healing journey begins to increase. Over time, grief gradually gives way to healing that eventually overtakes it.

Our grief journey still continues, but it becomes ever less prominent in our lives as we begin to engage in life again and the act of living, changing and growing promotes healing within us. In this way, the healing journey begins to become the dominant part of our lives; the grief journey is submerged "behind it," in a sense. This part of both journeys corresponds to the second part of the book in the Learning to Live Again and Reconstruction chapters.

Again, differently for each of us, we gradually move to a place of wellness. Our grief becomes much less a part of our daily lives and the healing becomes much more of what we are and do and this continues to progress as we begin to find, create, and live our new lives.

Wellness is the final part of the continuum and we keep moving towards it as we continue to grow and continue to heal. In the book, the Acceptance and Wellness chapters are about this part of the continuum.

At some point then, as healing turns into wellness, our bereavement also moves more strongly towards growth and life. There may always be an element of grief in our lives but it becomes less and less powerful with time. There may always be an element of healing as well since there are always new things to learn that can help us to heal ever more fully as wellness takes over in our lives.

So, during the course of our bereavement, all three journeys can occur on their own. They can also occur simultaneously as we travel through the overall journey that began with our bereavement and continues through healing into wellness and living fully however we can.

Visually, it might look something like this:

Grief becomes less over time...
       Healing grows over time...
              Wellness develops as healing grows stronger.........
                    Healing turns to wellness ...

How long does it take?

It takes as long as it takes! There is no timetable or calendar. Grief, healing and finding wellness progress at their own pace, differently for each of us. Also, as I wrote earlier, healing and grief appear to be fairly non-linear; sometimes we go forward and sometimes not, but we are always changing in some way even when it isn't obvious.

The one thing that may be a constant is that our grief does indeed change through time and it changes us through time as well. By our growing surrender to it, most times, it tends to becomes less severe, we learn and grow and move forward, each in our own way and at our own rate, towards healing and functional living. Maybe this is what wellness feels like.

Negative grief and mourning behaviors:

Just a brief thought here, there can be grief or mourning behaviors that may be the results of pain, anger or frustration within our grief that are loud or violent or hurtful to ourselves or others. There may be things that can happen that are intrusive on others that we should be aware of and perhaps seek professional help for, if our grief or mourning becomes too intense to navigate by ourselves.

❁

We are not our grief, We are grieving:

Some Affirmations:

This is something I learned from Andi during her cancer journey. She decided early on that she was not going to be her cancer. She was going to be herself living with cancer and she was going to go on living despite it and be herself as much as possible through it all.

What I learned was to apply that idea to the experience of grieving as: we are not our grief, we are grieving.

Grief can be one of the most overwhelming emotional turmoils we ever experience. It can feel like and be one of the most painful things we ever go through. But it's good to remember, even during the worst of the pain, that grief is something that is happening to us, but it isn't us. We are separate from our grief, and so while we experience it, we can also move through it and it can move through us. While we may be changed by it, we can still be growing, learning and healing through it all, even when we don't notice it happening.

Our grief may become all encompassing for a while, painful beyond relief for a while, but with time, we also begin to notice ourselves separate from it. We can become ourselves again, apart from the grief, honoring our loved ones in memory, and while we are changed by it, we are not our grief!

As we grieve, I think it is also important to always remember that again, there is no one way to grieve or mourn, nor is there one way to go through grief and mourning, nor is there a time table, nor a "should do" list, nor a calendar... How ever long it takes, that's how long it takes.

We grieve because we love:

Another important thing for us to consider and remember, especially early on is that it is our love and the ending of our lives with our loved ones that cause us to grieve. We miss them and all the interactions and time we spent together. We miss the things we did and said and were to each other, the things we will never get to do or the things we will never do again. We feel the sadness and loneliness of being without them filling their space in our daily lives.

For all these things and more, we experience deep sorrow and pain, feeling and believing that we will not be able to have any more time or experiences or love with our spouse or partner. And everything and every moment reminds of this. And it hurts! And it becomes the most wished for thing we have, if I could only have another hug or another day or...

Here's a verse and chorus from a song we wrote that captured those feelings pretty strongly I think.

Now there is empty,
now there is sadness,
now there is living all alone,

Now there is wishing,

with every breath I take,
for your somehow coming home.

...I am standing,
though I'm wracked with pain,
though my life has been shattered,
from us, into me, all alone...

from I Remain (© Howard and Andrea Adaire Fischer, 2020)

While we are not our grief, we do still grieve and mourn and something important I want to affirm here is: It's always OK to grieve!

Because there is no one way to do it, nor one right way to do it or experience it, you can do it in your own way and do it in your own time. It's not up to others to tell you how or when to grieve nor for anyone to tell you when your grieving should be ended.

When it's time to do something on your grief journey, you will know it, but it has to be when it feels right for you and not when somebody or some book or something you saw on the internet says you should do something or be something.

It's just different for each of us, and we need to follow our own timetable and our own hearts... And yet again, how ever long it takes, that's how long it takes.

Express your grief and mourning whenever you need to and whenever the flood comes and carries you away:

Since grief feelings come without warning and don't care where you are or what you are doing or who you're with, you can choose to express them when and where they strike you. You can let them happen and not fight them knowing that many times, maybe that's all you can do, you may have no choice. Just take a "grief moment" whenever and wherever you need to.

You also don't have to run from your grief because it hurts so badly; you can embrace it and experience it and remember that it is also a celebration of your love. We will talk more about these two ideas in another chapter.

In the end, this is your grief to experience. It is uniquely yours by the nature of your love and the life you shared with your loved one. No matter how difficult it seems, I think it is always good to do it your way, from your heart.

Some questions to ask yourself and think about:

- Does it help to think of being separate from your grief and not let it be who you are?

- Can you see a way to separate from your grief but still remain yourself within the grieving?

- Can you perhaps think of any examples of you and your grief being different and separate?

- What things do you miss most and do you see it as possible to learn to live without them in your daily lives?

- How might you begin to be able to do that and learn to fill some of those empty spaces?

- How do you feel about letting yourself grieve/mourn in public? Is there really a choice?

- What can you or do you do when grief comes over you in a public place?

- What do you hope for in your bereavement? Do you feel that those hopes are realistic?

- How can you use your hope to help you heal?

- What does healing mean to you in the sense of your grief?

- What would you like to learn or experience that would make you feel like you were healing?

- What will it take for you to realize hope and/or healing?

- Can you imagine wellness and if so, what does it, (will it) look like to you?

Chapter 2

Struggle vs Surrender

*N*avigating your grief:

This chapter contains some things to think about as you reach a point where you can begin to choose the path you will take on your own unique journey towards wellness.

Definitions:
The topic of "surrender" often holds a negative connotation. By definition, surrender means "to yield to the power or domination of another," and we often think of surrender as an aspect of wartime or intense conflict.

In the context of grief, surrender can take on another meaning. "Surrendering to your grief" means allowing yourself to be where you are at without judgment (as best as you can), to allow your emotions to be felt (after all feelings just want to be felt in the end), and to accept (in small steps) the reality of your life.

Surrender, in this more positive sense also means not fighting against your grieving. Surrender then becomes a process through which each person can find their own unique way.

It is very common in the early weeks and months of grief, even years for some, for a person to "fight" and "struggle against" their grief, trying to gain control and somehow defeat the overwhelming reality of their loss. Surrendering can bring about a sense of fear, of thoughts like; if I let myself feel the depth of my pain, it will swallow me forever, I will never come out of it or feel better.

Ironically, the opposite is usually true, when you confront and feel your grief head on, it is a step in processing your loss and helps you to accept the changes in your life and move forward little by little. It is normal to resist what is painful, but by surrendering and feeling your grief, you allow yourself to be where you are rather than wishing you were somewhere else, which is usually not a healthy way to cope in the long term.

I also want to normalize that, as I wrote earlier, we usually see in the earlier months of grief more difficulty in taking steps towards surrender, and further on in one's grief, it often becomes easier. If you are not ready to try this out, that is ok and you need to honor that need. (from Amanda Hillman, Pathways for Grief and Loss Counselor, 2021)

Resistance: the refusal to accept something, the attempt to prevent something by action or argument. The opposition to, hostility to, refusal, struggle or unwillingness to accept something or become something. Resistance is much the same as struggle in the context of grief and is the opposite of acceptance!

Waves of grief:

One of the most commonly expressed statements I've heard about grief from people who are grieving and in things I've felt and written about in my journal, is that rather than being a constant feeling, feelings of grief rise and fall and crash over us like waves at the shore. It is a powerful image to use in talking about grief, and we will look at it more deeply in Chapter Four.

So in that context, here's what I would like to consider in this chapter: should we fight our grief (struggle, resist) or not fight our grief (surrender) and go with the flow?

Three images from an old Oceanography Instructor:

1. If you've ever stood in the water on an ocean beach, especially after a storm when the waves are strong and high, the waves can knock you to your knees, they can put you on the ground and even roll you over and over as they wash back off the shore. When that happens, their strength is often so much greater than yours that all you can do is let it happen, roll with it and as each wave recedes and leaves you breathless on the sand, stand and become ready for the next wave.

It's the getting back up that is the challenge, especially when wave after wave knocks you down, and you become fatigued and start running out of strength and breath. But of course if you've been knocked down and are lying on the beach, you have to find a way to get back up and brace for the next wave.

2. If you are washed out to sea in a riptide, a seaward moving current that goes away from shore, it too is usually much stronger than you are. If you fight it, you will eventually tire and run out of energy, and by fighting, sometimes not have enough energy to make it back to shore.

But if you let the current take you, don't fight it, surrender to it and let it carry you with its energy and take you out towards the sea (even though that doesn't seem to be where you want to go), eventually the current will run out of energy. Once it does, you can use the strength and energy you didn't use fighting it to swim to its edge and then turn shoreward and swim back to shore.

3. When I first moved to Florida, I thought that if I lived on the coast, I would want to have the strongest reinforced concrete pilings I could find to build my house on so they would survive the winds and waves of a hurricane if it occurred.

I was surprised when I went to the coast that many of the homes built at the back of the beach had been and still were being built not on concrete pilings but on wood posts, much like telephone poles, that were driven deeply into the sand.

When I started trying to find out why, because it didn't make sense to me to use a less strong material, I found out that because concrete is not only strong but also rigid and inflexible, in the wind, it was actually often too resistant. It was not going to bend much at all, it was just going to rigidly stand there and eventually break and collapse because it couldn't be flexible.

Wood pilings, however, are like palm trees they flex and bend in the wind. While a house built on them may sway and shift, except during the most extreme conditions, the pilings don't usually fracture or shatter, they just bend and flex under the force of the wind and waves.

Another image to consider:

4. In electrical and computer systems, resistance reduces the flow of electricity and uses up energy. Resistance to the flow of electricity within the wiring is changed to heat as it moves through the

hardware and so degrades the amount of usable energy that moves through the system. Since it is a loss of energy along the way, the more resistance in the line, the less energy is available to run the system.

This is why your computer heats up as the energy flows and it processes data. The resistance takes some of the energy input and turns it into heat. The more resistance there is, the more heat is generated and the less energy remains for the computer to do its work.

What I learned:

Especially early in our journey, grief will take us were it will. It is its own strong current carrying us away from the shore of our familiar lives out towards the sea of a life unknown. It is a hurricane of emotion blowing through our life.

It has always been my personal inclination to be flexible and to try to go where the current takes me and to husband my strength for the learning and the growth the swim back to the shore of a new life as a widower will require of me.

Some reasons I chose to surrender to my grief:

I want to share a little more of my own journey here. My wife Andi survived stage-four breast cancer for 8 years. As I wrote in the first chapter, she decided early on that she was not going to be her cancer. She was going to be herself living with cancer and she was going to go on living despite it and be herself as much as possible through it all.

And she did. With grace and courage and an amazing strength I still look at with awe; she got up every day and took the time to do her hair, put on makeup, dress nicely and then faced the day with as much grace and clarity as she could no matter what was happening inside her even as the war between her cancer and her chemo-treatments went on and on.

I remember one year on her birthday, she'd had a chemo-treatment the day before but she got up on her birthday morning and said "let's go to the mountains today." So we packed up the car and drove an hour to Rocky Mountain National Park and walked trails up to a beautiful lake at about 9,000 feet elevation. She walked my butt off! She was ahead of me the whole way, and I had to work to keep up. I still honor her for her amazing strength and determination.

So with Andi as my example, I came to my own realization:

From my journal sometime early in the first few months of my bereavement:

"You don't fight to the end as hard as Andi fought only to have your husband wimp out and give up or run away because it hurts to have lost her. The message to me is to also fight to the end of my strength in my own way against my own pain and try to honor Andi's fight by doing mine with as much grace as she did hers."

Instead of fighting it as if it was an illness like cancer, however, I would surrender to it and let it wash over me. I would face it head on and experience it as it was happening but still remain myself within it.

I know that not everyone's spouse or partner got to fight to the end. Some were taken quickly or suddenly, but I think that the lesson still applies. At some point, when we are ready, we will all need to move forward. At some point we will need to "stop drowning in our sadness," to have what I call a "phoenix moment" and begin to rise out of the ashes of our grief. We can honor our spouses and ourselves by the courage, strength and manner in which we face our grief and build our new lives.

Another reason I surrendered to it:

The first year of my bereavement, as it is for everyone, was a year of firsts. First birthday, first anniversary, first holidays... Especially for the first Christmas, my kids and grandkids really wanted me to come to Florida to be with them, so I wasn't lonely and didn't have to face it alone.

That was a really confusing time for me, I knew they were concerned for me and wanted to help me but inside I just wanted to stay home and experience it, to just see what happened and how I felt and in a way, to still be home and spend the time as Andi and I had usually done.

I have to be honest as I'm writing this, and say that at the time, in the pain and devastation of my early bereavement, I never even considered that they might have needed me to be there for them in their own bereavement. I'm hoping that we've talked enough and shared enough over the years since, that I was able to help them with the needs of their grief as I became more able and aware down the road.

I ended up having to schedule a meeting with a grief counselor to help me talk it out and figure out the right thing for me to do. And I chose in the end to not go to Florida and to stay home and face and experience what grieving though the holidays felt like. I did the same thing on Andi's birthday and on our anniversary.

I learned some things from those experiences:

The first time these important things and events happen and in a sense each new day of our grief journeys as well, is the only time we will experience these feelings and emotions in their full, raw and unfiltered nature.

They will probably cause you to hurt, maybe more than you ever have before. They will most likely cause you to change. But if you face them head on and let them wash over you, if you surrender to them, you will know, without a doubt, what it was like and you will have had the experience. And when they have passed, like the waves, you will know that you were strong enough and that you are still standing.

If you choose to run away from the experiences, if you deny them or try to avoid them, then you won't experience them or learn from them at that point in your journey. And that's an OK choice to make if it's what you need to do. But consider, if you don't deal with them the first time around, then the next time around, like the second Christmas for example, you will probably still have to face them. But then they will be at a year removed from the event and your reactions and your experience and what you may learn will be different than they would have been had you experienced them the first time.

We only get one "first time" for each moment and each event in our lives as well as in our grief journeys. Each first time experience is unique and a unique opportunity to grow and learn even if it is a painful and disorienting experience. If we choose surrender, in the end we will have done it and not have to wonder later what it would have been like or fear it yet again the next time it comes up in our lives.

Though they were very difficult and painful for me to go through, my memories of those events have since turned into treasures for my having been there and gone through them and for my having seen what the strength and breadth of our love brought me in the depths of my grief. I wouldn't trade a single experience now, difficult and painful as they were at the time.

No matter how difficult it seemed, I found that if I surrendered to my grief, by doing it my own way, from my heart, my surrender had great power to help me on my road to hope, healing and wellness.

❀

Honoring our loved ones by trying to grieve with purpose and intent:

What would our loved ones want us to do or be as we grieve? Can we honor our loved ones by giving them the gift of us grieving and learning and growing as graciously as possible, with as much strength as possible, with as much courage as possible, however that looks for us?

Since we grieve because we love, as we grieve then, we have an opportunity to do it as another act of love. When we are ready, we can choose to face our grief with purpose. We can choose to experience and face it in ways that honor our loved ones. We can accept it and surrender to it and move through it to honor our spouses and partners and the love we shared while we learn to stand and live again, on our own.

Again, this is another topic we will explore a number of times later in the book.

❀

Surrender:

This chapter is based on how I chose and was moved to act especially during the early part of my grief journey. I am here today, perhaps at the ending of my grief journey, still standing, functioning and continuing to build a new life that honors Andi and is much more rich than I ever would have expected.

I believe much of that is due, for me, to the early choice I made to surrender to my grief and face it head on, to allow it to knock me to my knees, and to learn, slowly, to get back up and stand, ready for the next wave to break.

From that surrender, I was able to build a strength within myself that has allowed me to move forward, to move through my grief and begin to find wellness in my life. Rather than squandering my strength fighting and struggling against it again and again, I believe that facing it allowed me to move through it more easily (although not less painfully) and more gracefully because I wasn't resisting it.

"I remain here standing, though I am lonely, I'm still living, and I'm still me!"

From I Remain (© Howard and Andrea Adaire Fischer 2020).

It's your journey. Think about how you will approach your grief. Will you choose to struggle or surrender or maybe choose a little bit of both?

A few more questions to think about connected to this chapter:

- Is it better for you to be rigid and inflexible (struggling against and/or denying your grief)?

- Is it better for you to be more malleable and bend under the force that is applied to you by your grief (surrendering to your grief)?

- Can you think of other places or situations where surrender is a positive force that you might use as a model for applying it to your grieving?

- Where are you at in the process of learning to accept what has happened?

- Are you struggling against what has happened and against your grieving or beginning to find acceptance of what has happened and the grief it has caused you to feel? Have you begun to surrender and face (accept) the changes in your life and your grief?

Chapter 3

Spiritual Connections

WITH YOU IN SPIRIT,
ALWAYS..
ANDREA ADAIRE

KAMI SPIRIT, ESTES PARK, CO.

SILVERDREAMSTUDIO
LOVELAND, CO.

To begin this chapter, I want to define another word I use frequently and then share two stories about things that happened to me along the way to help set the stage for the discussion to come.

The first story is about a defining moment that changed my life and in many ways created the path my grieving and my healing took from that point forward. The second happened three and three quarter years into my bereavement, as I was going through the house and adjusting our physical space to reflect my living there by myself.

Confluence defined as I use it:

Through the years of my grief journey, there have been numerous times when I experienced what I came to call confluences. These were times when I had a thought or a feeling, and at that exact moment, something happened that was totally unexpected, but at that moment, things came together at the perfect time and place. I gradually began to see that those moments were Andi sort of tapping me on the shoulder and saying, "I'm still here."

My favorite moment happened on a day when I was at the cemetery talking to Andi and I got the strong feeling to turn around and look behind me. I did, and standing there, no more than three yards away was a beautiful buck deer. He lifted his head from the grass and just looked at me. Whoa!

So I turned back around, thought about getting my phone out to take a picture and when I turned back, the deer was gone. Gone, nowhere in sight. I cried, and I said thank you and let it become another strong part of the process of suspending my disbelief that I will talk about later in the chapter.

I told a friend at that time too, as an example of what I meant by confluences; "its not that a deer was in the forest, it's that I was there at that exact moment to see it walk out from behind the tree that was special."

Story of the love flower:

For what turned out to be our last Valentines day together, I bought Andi a flowering plant with the glittery word LOVE written on a stick placed in the pot. As with most flowering plants, once the first blooms faded, it just became another leaf-plant. While it stayed healthy and grew new leaves from time to time, it didn't flower again.

After Andi passed in April of that year, our wedding anniversary came three weeks later and I was, as you might imagine, not doing very well. Without my noticing, the "love plant" had been quietly growing, and on the very day of our anniversary, it opened a new bright red flower. It was surely a gift from Andi, a flower to say I love you and to make my day a bit easier.

I took it then as a communication, a way of her letting me know she was ok, and that our love was still strong. I took that thought and held it close and it became the basis of many things I began to see and experience that were outside the normal but that I began to realize were ways Andi was letting me know she was still with me in spirit and still part of my life.

There are a few more parts to this story. After that first time, the plant sent out a flower on every important day during the entire first year. It flowered on her birthday, on our anniversary, and amazingly, each year on her passing day! It went on like that through all the years of my grief journey.

As an example, we had passed the four year mark at the end of April of 2020 and so another wedding anniversary day was also approaching. Once again, a flower opened on the "love plant" and was there, bright and beautiful in the morning when I got up on our anniversary day. Love across the veil as I like to say…

Story of the Always Print:

The second story happened just before the start of the fourth year of our journey. As I was cleaning out file cabinets getting rid of old papers that were no longer needed, I came across a file folder with a large number of pictures in it. These were mainly 8x10 prints of photos I had taken and many of them had words on them that Andi had written of thoughts, feelings and expressions of our love. I had at some point added her words to the images and then printed them. And then they got put in a file and mostly forgotten during the last year or so of her illness.

Sorting the files came at a difficult time for me. It was during the first time I had really gone through things from our life and began to sort and change and remove what was no longer needed. As I was going through the photos, some brought tears as I remembered where we were when we took the photos and also from the feelings generated when I read her words.

But then I came upon one I didn't remember doing. I remembered the picture, but didn't remember putting it into the framework it was in, and I definitely didn't remember the words Andi had written to go with the image.

But there, below the picture, set there for me to find, were the words "With you in Spirit, Always." There it was, a message, a gift, and a very clear and understandable statement of something she knew way before I did and something left for me to find as we were approaching the four year mark. It was there waiting for me when I needed reassurance and strength yet again to go forward, to continue to live and grow and to understand that love does go on forever, it just takes different forms and requires different ways of communicating.

And I have to add that it got even more amazing as I was searching my computer photo files for a copy of that image to include in a blog post. I couldn't find it! I searched all the possible places I would have put it and all the other folders of images I could think of and it plain wasn't there. So at that point, I stopped looking, realizing I had no part in it at all and just said thank you to my sweet wife for sending me something so special, in such a special way and for having it there waiting for me on a day when I needed to see it.

Spiritual ideas to consider:

The spiritual experiences I'm going to write about here may or may not happen to you. They are not required to happen. There are no judgements associated with whether you have experienced any of these things or not. They are just possibilities. They have been reported by many people but surely not by all. Their meaning is always open to how you interpret them if indeed you do experience them.

My purpose here is just to suggest that if you do experience things like this, that you can consider them in a way you perhaps have not in the past. If you do experience them, hopefully, they can be used to help in your growth and healing. If you do not experience them or you do not find the explanations that I propose resonate with you, that is fine as well.

We all have to find our own way through our grief and what works for you is the important thing for your growth and healing. These ideas are what I took from my own experiences and how I interpreted them is how they seemed to be for me as I was experiencing them. I share them in hopes that if you are trying to understand similar experiences you can use what I learned to help you with your understanding.

I've used three terms often in this discussion and I want to let you know what they mean to me when I use them since they may have very different meanings to others.

Spirit and soul: The animating force within us that is also who we are. Soul is that animating force when it is within a person in the material world and spirit is when that force is no longer animating a body but exists as a separate entity none-the-less. I also use spirit as a larger idea for perhaps a composite consciousness that exists wherever spirits exist.

The veil: The boundary between the material world and wherever spirits exist.

Hope, Faith and Belief - connections that end, connections that remain:

There are many places where the spiritual nature of life and death are discussed and written about and most religions have very strong pictures of the part spirit (soul) plays in one's life and how the spirit (soul) behaves and where it goes after it is free of its earthly body. It is not for this discussion to talk about any of those things in a religious way. My only purpose here is to share my own understanding of spirit based on what I've seen, heard and experienced during my bereavement and to propose some thoughts to help you perhaps recognize that a manifestation and communication of spirit might be possible within the context of your own grief.

We are our spirits:

If you believe that there is an animating force within us that is who we are and that it is usually called soul or spirit when we talk about it, then it seems possible that who we are isn't limited by the body that surrounds it. If spirit is really who we are, when our bodies die, our spirits are then free of the constraints of the material world and are free to move onward. Again, where they go and how or why that happens is usually in the realm of religion and not for this discussion. What is important in this context is that if who we are is not just our bodies, and if we are truly our spirits or souls, then the passing of our bodies in no way ends the existence of the essence that is ourselves.

Dreams, visions, voices from across the veil:

The passing of a spouse, or partner, of a parent, or child, or a close, special friend can often be a reality altering experience. Sometimes, in our extreme sadness, disorientation and emotional pain, it may seem like we can see a bit more of the universe than we normally do. Sometimes we seem to be able to see or hear our loved ones reaching out to us in dreams or visions or voices. Perhaps instead of these things just being a product of our grief or imagination, we actually can experience different things during and through our bereavement that we may not be able to do under more ordinary circumstances.

Perhaps in a sense, the veil to the spirit world thins with the passage of a soul through it and creates an increase in permeability and our connection to our loved ones provides a pathway through which we can experience things that we may not be able to do otherwise. The thinning of the veil between the everyday world and the world of soul, between the material world and the spirit world may allow us to experience dreams, visions and voices, that are messages if you will, from our loved ones.

Suspending our disbelief, a new way to look at the world:

If we experience these moments of perceptual change, if we see or hear more than we are used to and are experiencing things we may not understand or may not have believed in, we have a choice. We can deny what we are perceiving and hold tight to the world as we knew it or we can suspend our disbelief and accept that the world is a larger and stranger place than we thought.

If we choose to, we can come to see that there are things that are possible that we may not be able to explain or fit into the seemingly rational way of looking at the world we may have grown up with or have lived with all our lives to this point. We may not be able to explain them but by suspending our disbelief, we can take the dreams, visions and voices and listen to them and accept that we feel, hear and see them. We can be joyful and honored that our love and our connection to our loved ones was so strong that it could open these pathways and allow these messages to reach in both directions across the veil.

The thinning of the veil between the material world and the spirit world with the passage of a soul across it, as part of the emotional turmoil of our grief, may actually allow us to experience these messages from our loved ones, not as hallucinations, but as actual transcendent experiences, as reality, not illusion.

Love flows both ways:

I think that for most of us, we can agree that our spouses or partners loved us as we loved them and throughout our lives together, the love that we shared built a spiritual connection between us. If you believe as it says in so many different places, that when you die, you are reunited with your loved ones, then they need to be able to recognize you, spirit to spirit, and you need to be able to recognize them, spirit to spirit when you are reunited. I believe that we learn that recognition not of our bodies but of our spirits all throughout our lives together and through the love that we build and share.

So also, our loved ones would not want us to be hurting or sad or lonely as much as we would not want to be those things ourselves. We surely would not have wanted that to be true for them if the roles were reversed.

So, should it not also be possible that they can and would want to reach back across the veil to give us reassurance if they could? Would they not want to sooth us, to comfort us, to hold us with spirit arms just to let us know they are safe and at peace? Would they not want to let us know that their spirit is still with us, that they are and will be a part of us forever?

New ways to communicate:

Remember the two stories I began with? Is it possible to accept all these new possibilities and take the communications we receive and see them as a gift and a connection and a way of communicating that was not available to us before?

I have seen that we can learn the language of it; we can come to see the presence of our loved ones in moments when things we don't expect to happen surprise us with new meanings. We can see them in moments of confluence when everything lines up and comes together.

We can slowly come to truly believe that our spirits are who we really are and that spirit is eternal. We can come to believe that spirits change worlds and locations, put on and off bodies as if they were clothing, but spirit, soul, and thus the essence of our loved ones, is always there, just across the veil. Sometimes, the veil is thin or permeable, and we can still communicate, just using other ways, other "languages" if you will.

For me, these realizations and experiences have been a comfort and have become an integral part of the new life I have been building. They are often a source of joy and wonder that fills my world with hope and healing. Suspending my disbelief and opening myself up to spirit has enriched my life by expanding my view of the universe to allow me to see it as a much larger place than I once believed it to be.

As I've intimated in other places, Andi and I have also learned to share at another level, beyond just what may happen during the shake up of reality that can be a part of our early grief. Later in the journey, again when I wasn't expecting it, sometimes when we were out walking and I was talking to her, I could feel her begin to "speak with my voice" and to tell me things I need to know or learn. Things I didn't know or understand that were answers to questions I was asking or visions of the path I might need to take going forward.

I know very definitely when that happens now, when the tone and the feeling of it is suddenly very Andi, and it is very different from my usual way of thinking or talking. And so it is another sharing across the veil and the way in which many of the things in this book came into being as Andi's contribution to it. It is also connected to the gift story below, the images in the book, and to how the music story in Chapter 6 unfolded. For us, it has become a conversation again and not just a monologue.

❀

A gift on the Spirit Wind:

I'm writing this on Andi's Day, the five year anniversary of the day her spirit was set free of its earthly bounds. I want to share the most recent chapter in the growth of this amazing journey and share some things that have been happening during the fourth and fifth year of my bereavement.

Towards the end of the time of isolation that COVID brought into the world in 2020, and through into 2021, not only communication, but a creative sharing began growing between us, and it has opened up some things I never would have believed were possible.

As background, I want to share that Andi was a natural musician; she could sit at a piano or organ and play the music she heard in her soul for hours. It was always amazing to listen to her just letting that music pass through her, to her fingers, to the keyboard, and then to my wondering ears. Unfortunately, we were never able to record any of her music and all I had was a memory.

At that time, I also began listening to meditative music, music that had been created for yoga and meditation practice and for finding calmness and aiding sleep. When I first heard it, I remember thinking "this is the music Andi was playing so many years ago;" she was hearing that spiritual and peaceful music and bringing it into the world.

As part of the things I learned during the first years of my bereavement, I learned to do digital recording. I had also started to explore creating MIDI music, the use of "software instruments" to create music in an entirely digital environment on the computer, mostly using a keyboard that generates digital notes that the computer translates into instrument sounds.

My biggest issue was that while I do play guitar, I don't really play the keyboard. I don't have much of a feel for it and certainly have no technique for making it sound like music.

But, one day I sat down and got everything hooked up and plugged into the keyboard. Before I began to try playing, I was thinking about Andi's music, her chords and melodies and how they remained in my memory. I hit the record button and just started to let my fingers move over the keys. After a few notes I could feel Andi's spirit take over my hands, and the music changed from my stumbling notes to a series of chords and a calming and peaceful melody.

I sat there in awe and knew it was Andi's music coming through. Tears started flowing, and I just welled up with emotion at what was happening and the possibility that I could be the instrument through which her music could again enter into the material world, a sharing and a gift across the veil.

It was just a short recording that first time but it was the start of something that has kept me in awe of what has been happening for a while now. I am still learning the processes of mixing, editing and mastering the music, but each time we do another recording, I seem to learn a little more.

There are some recordings that are pure Andi and others, where somehow the music I hear has also become incorporated in what we have created. I've learned to create a background sound for her melodies to rest upon that supports the feeling of peace and calm they contain. Most recently, I believe we have begun to join our creative selves and both be part of the music as it comes through.

It is my hope that they are peaceful and calming for you if you listen, and that they are something you can find peace and enjoyment in. They are definitely a gift across the veil that it is my blessing to be a part of, to be able to bring Andi's music here to share and for us to be able to create together.

I've posted the music on our website flowersfromandrea.com and you can listen to it there if you are interested.

❀

Some questions to consider:

- If you have not had any of these experiences, how does reading about them impact you?

- Would you be willing to "suspend your disbelief" in some way if it meant you had to change how you view the world? What if doing that helped you to find some healing?

- If you have had any of these experiences, do you see them as hallucinations or do you think they are indeed real communications from your loved one?

- No matter whether you have had them or not, do you see these as possible and real or are they too strange and "out there"?

- What do you think these things mean in the context of your grief?

Chapter 4

Waves of Grief

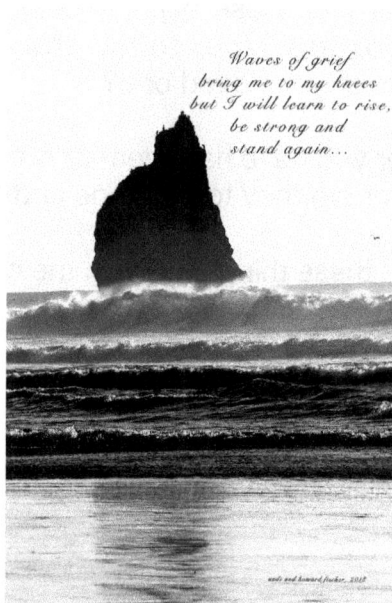

*Waves of grief
bring me to my knees
but I will learn to rise,
be strong and
stand again...*

O ne of the most commonly expressed statements I've heard about grief from people who are grieving, in support group meetings and in looking back at things I've written in my journal during my own grief journey, is that rather than being a constant feeling, feelings of grief rise and fall and crash over us like waves at the shore.

From my journal:

"My missing you washes over me uncontrollably on its own time and tide and when it does it sears my mind and body with grief and pain and longing and what do I do now's until it subsides and ebbs for another unknowable length of time until it turns and again washes over me and I cry another part of my million tears."

As part of that image I also want to add that: Waves of Grief = Waves of Love!

Each time a wave of grief crashes over you, mixed with the pain and feelings of loss and sadness, try to remember that we grieve because we love.

Going to your knees under the onslaught of the waves. Learning to get back up:

As I wrote about in Chapter 2, if you've ever stood in the water on an ocean beach, especially after a storm when the waves are strong and high, the waves can knock you to your knees, they can put you on the ground and roll you over and over as they wash back off the shore. When that happens, their strength is so much greater than yours, all you can do is let it happen, roll with it and as the wave recedes and leaves you breathless on the sand, try to stand and become ready for the next wave.

It's the getting back up that is the challenge, especially when wave after wave knocks you down and you become fatigued and start running out of strength and breath. But of course you still have to get back up and brace for the next wave. Does fatigue in this example perhaps seem like the feelings of hopeless we may feel in our early grief?

I've heard people say that "this hurts worse than anything I've ever experienced. No one can be hurting as much as I am."

It can feel that bad! Early in the grief journey, grief is in control. The waves come so fast and the hurt comes at such a visceral level that it is almost totally emotional and uncontrollable. It can make us sick or sick-feeling all day long and for day after day. It will almost surely make us cry at times like we will never be able to stop. It can keep us from eating and sleeping well and it generally messes with everything in our lives as wave after wave crashes over us. It can feel that bad and that hopeless!

That level of pain happens to a lot of us in our early grief and while ours may feel like it's the worst ever and becomes almost an isolating thing, we can also find ways to come together and to tell our stories. We can share that pain, dilute it by the sharing and find some relief by letting it be expressed outside of ourselves and knowing that we are not alone in what we are feeling and going through.

Hope vs. Hopelessness: looking for some light:

As I suggested above, grief can definitely cause feelings of hopelessness, especially when the waves come over us day after day, week after week, month after month. It sometimes feels like we will never get any relief and the pain will go on forever.

Sometimes that hopelessness can make it very hard to find the will to care about much of anything at all, to doubt that there is a good reason out there for us to even bother to try. It is another part of the inertia we will talk more about in Chapter 8 that, as we look at our shattered lives, at the loss of not only our love but of our futures, that we often can't see a reason to look toward the future at all. It's hard in that time to not descend into some pretty heavy hopelessness and see no reason to do much of anything.

But I believe that it's important to remember that since we are not our grief, we are grieving, it may well be our grieving that makes us feel that way. It may be a form of mental inertia.

If nothing else, I believe that our loved ones would want us to carry on, to find new reasons to live and grow and maybe more importantly, if the roles were reversed, we would want those things for them!

I believe it's important to hold on through those bleak times, through the winter of our grieving, to do the work and to move forward in small steps as we can. I believe that it is important to slog through the snow no matter how tired we feel and how hopeless it looks. Until one day, out of seemingly nowhere, we see a small fire burning in the distance that we can head toward, embrace and allow its heat and light to begin to warm us and heal us. To let us find the strength within ourselves to survive, and not just to survive, but to begin to grow and live again.

I believe in hope and healing and doing what ever it takes to build that within our shattered hearts, emotions and lives. I believe our loved ones would want us to do so. As one of the people in a support group said to me some years ago, her husband told her at the end of his life, "live for us both and don't give up on living with all your strength."

Speaking from a perspective of almost seven years out and from attending many support group meetings as well, I can say for myself and for a large number of bereaved spouses and partners that I've talked with, that with time, the waves do become less high. They also come less often and we start being able to catch our breaths between waves. We can slowly move from grief being in control of our lives to beginning to take control back into our own hands. We can see healing begin to rise within us.

Further along, if not the sun, we can at least begin to see the light behind the clouds and the promise that some day, some time, some how, the clouds might actually part and some light will come back into our lives. We can begin to feel that the storm will finally pass and that gentle, calming swells of life will replace the intensity and turbulence of the waves of grief. We can start to live again and begin building our (new) lives.

Hiding your Grief, Hiding from your Grief or Expressing your Grief:

We all have choices, conscious or not, about how we will deal with our grieving even if we feel out of control, especially early on.

We can choose to be (seemingly) strong and stoic and try to hide (struggle against) our feelings of grief and not express them. We can try to control them and keep them to and maybe from ourself, locked away inside.

We can also hide from our grief, get super busy and try to put the feelings off by doing a lot of other things because we hurt so badly. We may even think they have gone away...

When we do any type of avoidance however, like struggling against, hiding or hiding from our grief, my experience and that of others I've talked to, is that the feelings of grief don't really go away. What we've done is just let the feelings and emotions become hidden and because we are not dealing with them, they remain unresolved and can build up inside us where they still remain even if we don't think so since we haven't learned the things we need to learn.

They may also get even more intense tucked away inside us until they find a way to come out sometime later down the road. Sometimes they explode as anger, sometimes they just build up and return to the surface with even more overwhelming pain than before.

In that light, I have seen people return to support group meetings after a few years of hiding from their grief in one way or another and they were often more hurt and confused than they were at the beginning of their journeys. Because they never dealt with the grief early on, it sat in the background and actually seemed to grow within them until it finally made its way back into their full awareness where they finally had to deal with it anyway.

As I wrote about in Chapter 2, a third choice we have is to face our grief (surrender to it) as and when it comes over us. Grief is part of life and love and we are here to experience it all and learn from it as part of our journey.

Express your grief and mourning whenever you need to and whenever the flood comes and carries you away:

Since waves of grief often come without warning and don't care where you are or what you are doing or who you're with, you often have to express them when and where they strike you. You can let them happen and not fight them knowing that many times, maybe that's all you can do, you may have no choice. Just take a "grief moment" whenever and wherever you need to.

You also don't have to run from your grief when it hurts so badly, you can embrace it and experience it and remember that grief is also a celebration of your love. We will talk more about these two ideas in Chapter 10.

Doing Things, Learning Things, Small Mitigations:

Often our grief feelings are so intense, we may have great difficulty dealing with them all at once or day after day. At times we may need to try to find ways to put them aside temporarily if we can, to get busy doing something or focusing on something else to help us put them off for just a little while. We can all use an "emotional day off". Even an hour or two off can help.

We all can be helped by taking some time away from our grief if we can find it, to let ourselves absorb and process what is happening in our grieving without thinking or feeling the intensity of it. This is a theme I will come back to many times, especially in the parts of the book that talk about reconstruction.

I personally looked to old hobbies from earlier in my life to fill those moments away from my grieving and to take me out of my grief for a bit. I also began learning new things as extensions of those activities that let me concentrate and focus on something away from my grief.

I chose to do something active and creative for my bit of relief time but probably listening to music or watching an absorbing movie or TV show would bring the same distraction. For many people, reading seems to require almost too much concentration early on but if that is your go to, if it works, it works.

I will say though, that learning new things engages so much of your attention and helps your mind stay active that therein lies an added benefit of more active vs. more passive activity. Again, this is just my personal preference and it's what worked for me.

Sometimes it helps to just get out and do things, alone if you feel comfortable with that or in small groups of friends or family. When you feel able to, spending time actively engaged in life, even if its only for a few hours each day, is a strong and effective way to begin the process of moving forward and stepping outside your grief. It's a time when you are not actively grieving and when you are giving yourself a break from the intensity that constantly grieving can bring.

This is not the same as the idea of "hiding from your grief" that we talked about above. What I'm talking about here is an active attempt to begin the process of living again while still acknowledging your grief. In that way, it can definitely be a positive part of the reconstruction process. I've written more about hiding from your grief in Chapter 10.

Whatever works for you is good and if it helps, go at it!

But, if what you are doing doesn't work and you find yourself not moving forward in a reasonable amount of time, you might want to try something else... Sitting on the couch or staying in bed and staring out into space and letting your grief overwhelm you day after day doesn't offer much to help you move forward to find hope, healing and growth.

Going to work if you need to or choose to may actually be healing and beneficial in providing that temporary break we need from our grieving. The waves may still come over us at work, but when we are engaged in our job and focused on the needs of doing our job correctly and well, we can be, for that time, outside our grief.

As with the other examples here, the "time off" from grieving is also a time when we can process some of the things that have been happening to us that we can't do when the waves are crashing.

Sharing the journey - grief shared helps dilute its intensity and helps us with our healing:

Telling your story is important:

This is one of the reasons we have support groups! One of the most valuable things I experienced in the early part of my grief journey was coming to support group meetings and both listening to other people tell their grief stories and being able to tell my own.

Hearing from people at different places along the way, a few months or even a number of years into the process, gave me ideas, things to think about and new ways to understand what was happening to me. One of the most important parts of the experience was that it let me know I wasn't alone and that sharing my grief would help to dilute it over time and that what was happening to me wasn't unique. It helped me begin to open to my healing journey as well.

Becoming each others "Friends in Grief" :

Because of our fairly single-minded attention to the needs of Andi's cancer journey, I essentially knew no one in our community besides a few nurses and doctors at the local Cancer Center. One of the early things I had to learn in my grief journey was how to make friends and somehow figure out where to find the people to make friends with. I've told the story of that journey in Chapter 11.

The ideas expressed below are another of the very important parts of what getting together a group of bereaved spouses and partners can lead to. They are based on something that happened to a group of us who were in a support group together. In an unplanned, organic growth, it blossomed into a powerful way for people in the group to grow and move forward into life again. I have put a description of the process as it happened to us and some ideas you might use to build such a community in your own lives in Chapter 11.

It may not be obvious, especially early in our journeys, but in a support group, as we listen and share our grief stories and the pain and sadness we feel, we are learning about each other and building strong bases on which friendships can develop. As we help each other to work through our grief, we are also building the foundations upon which our new lives will rest.

In most situations when we meet new people, it takes quite a lot of time to get to know them well. Relationships tend to build slowly over time in small bits of shared information, in finding commonalities, in learning likes and dislikes and at some level an almost intuitive resonance that keeps us coming back and learning more about each other.

At some point we have enough shared experiences that our relationship becomes a friendship and if both people are willing to give and take in relatively equal amounts, that friendship can grow and expand through our lives.

The key difference here is the time it takes to build a friendship. It usually isn't quick and most times slowly evolves as we get to know someone, sometimes over years.

In a support group, we tend to learn a lot about people in their most vulnerable places in a pretty short time. When we get together to share our grief stories we often tell the group very personal and intense feelings and things about ourselves that we would ordinarily not do until we have known someone for a very long time. Sometimes we share things we might never have shared with anyone in other circumstances.

Because of this almost artificial speeding up of the information transfer we are able to bridge the gap from stranger to friend much more quickly. Instead of looking for commonality, we know we have one very important thing in common, we all share a bereavement and the results of that bereavement on our lives. We immediately understand that about each other in ways that others who have not experienced grief of this type can probably never truly understand.

So, what we have done and are doing in the community of bereaved spouses and partners I routinely interact with is to build, and build on, those friendships and bonds. As time has passed and old friends and relationships have changed or fallen away because of our changed lives, these new "friends in grief" have become the core of the people we are now journeying forward with.

Our social lives, our conversations, and our interactions are all building out of these friendships. We will always have that basic commonality of "I get it. I know how you are feeling" that creates a comfort and familiarity no matter our backgrounds or beliefs. We all are bereaved and we can all help each other in the process of hope and healing.

And we are indeed becoming friends!

Crying and Hugging are OK:

We are all often brought to tears by the intensity of our emotions. I feel strongly that we all need to feel free to express the emotions behind those tears as well as the tears themselves when and where we need to.

One of the things a group of fellow travelers offers us when we meet is a safe place to cry. A place where everyone knows why we cry and that we often can't really control it and that we also need to do it. And hugs are a way of saying thanks to each other for the sharing, the understanding, the help, and the dilution of our pain by its sharing.

If you can, it can be a very positive thing to connect with others who share this journey and let each other know we are there to help each other in what ever way we can. I sincerely hope that when the need for social distancing is reduced or ended and it is safe, we can remember to hug again, that we can overcome our fears and reach out for the very important comfort of physical touch.

Getting other help:

At the end of this chapter, I again want to remind anyone who reads this to please consider seeking out professional counseling if dealing with your grief begins to seem too overwhelming. Many of us were caregivers in some way during our lives, so now, if you need to, please consider letting someone help you in your need as you may have helped others in theirs.

If people have been surviving grief and sharing their journeys for as long as there has been people and grief, then we can (and will) survive as well.

Questions:

- How do the waves of grief happen to you? What does it feel like?

- Do the waves feel differently if you have been grieving for a while?

- How do you react when a wave overtakes you?

- Can you cry and express your grief whenever you need to?

- Have you felt hopelessness while trying to see a path going forward or of finding a way of dealing with the changes in your life?

- Can you find ways to go forward despite feeling hopeless sometimes?

- Do you think your responsibility to others is an important component of the healing process?

- How might you begin to overcome hopelessness if you are feeling it?

- Do you feel like you may be hiding from or hiding your grief?

- How might you look to change that if you choose to?

Chapter 5

Dealing with the Holidays and Other Stressful Event Days - Creating Intent Statements for the New Year

To everything there is a season...

*D*ealing with the larger waves of grief that often accompany holidays and other special but also stressful events, days and times during the year:

Holidays and other important or significant days during the year are always special and important times in our lives. In our grief however, the specialty of those days can be transformed into especially painful and difficult.

Particularly during our "year of firsts," the first time these days occur during our grief journeys, our grief is often expanded and opened wider and somehow made more unbearable. In some ways, how we deal with these events can set the stage for how we proceed through our early grief and be a strong part of how we eventually make the transition to healing and wellness.

In a sense, holiday events are waves of grief of their own. They are times when the gentle swells of our days and the large breakers of our grief are even higher and more chaotic. In an image I've used before, the waves can bring us to our knees and set us rolling in the surf until we begin to grow short of breath and fear that we will not be able to rise again and begin the process of moving forward once more.

Some special, significant and difficult days:

- Christmas
- Thanksgiving
- Their Passing Day
- Their Birthday
- Your birthday
- Anniversary
- Family weddings
- Valentines day
- Veterans Day
- Kids/grandkids birthdays
- Others ?

As I've written about in Chapter 2, there are two times during our grief journeys when these significant days come up, the first time and all the rest of the times. There's a Grateful Dead song that begins, "The first days are the hardest days...." I think it applies here to both our grief and the days within it that have particular emotional meaning.

There is only one first time for each event! It's usually the most intense and poignant.

We all have to go through each "significant" day without our loved ones for the first time and we have almost nothing to hold onto or cling to as the waves begin to rise and try to sweep us away.

Dealing with those days is much like all the other parts of our grief we have to deal with. As I've written about in a number of places, it is always my inclination to face the moments of my grief head on and experience whatever they have to put me though, and more importantly, what they have to teach me.

These firsts are almost always especially painful but the experience can be and can become a very important and significant part of our healing.

Facing or dealing with the holidays, choosing how we will proceed through them, deciding if we will do things we have always done or if we will change how we do them are all parts of the journey that it is our individual choice to do. Whether to keep, change or modify long term traditions is also our choice.

Sometimes it may work best to just hunker down and let the waves wash over us on those significant days that we shared, especially those that were particularly special to just us and our spouses or partners. But in the end, its experimental in a way, you have to do the things that feel right to you and experience what they bring and how they effect you individually and then decide how you want to go on.

Do you want to change or keep things the same, do you want to honor the memories by doing things as you always did or do you need to change things because the emotions of keeping things the same without your loved one with you are too much to go through?

I've told the story of my first Christmas in Chapter 2, and that story is an illustration of some choices we can make and of the way I personally decided to face and experience these things in my own journey.

I unfortunately don't have instructions to share with you about what you can or should do on these days. Its just another place where you have to find a way to do it that meets your own needs and your own inclinations.

Usually too, there are other people involved on those days. There are family and friends who also have needs and feelings within their grief that we may have to find ways of dealing with and hopefully respecting.

So, how do you want to go on, especially after the first time? Do you want to hold on to old traditions, break old traditions, make new traditions or perhaps, do nothing at all? Would you rather have what you do change each year so you can adapt what you do to each season, event and holiday? Would it be good to fill your changing needs and wants with changing responses as your grief journey changes through time?

How can you also respect and possibly meet the needs of others of your family and friends that may be very strong and grief filled as well. What if their needs are different than yours? Can you or should you compromise?

I'm not sure how often we think about how the grief of our spouses or partners passing affects our families and friends either.

I've heard the general comment that each person in a family reacts differently and we should be careful not to expect the same reaction across all the people who are effected. Since they are all different people, we really should expect that their grief is different as well. I personally know that each of my children dealt with it differently and so did my grandchildren who were old enough to understand what had happened.

It is really the same thing I've learned from listening to many of the grief journeys I hear in support group meetings, each of us grieve in our own way and in our own time. The biggest thing I feel that is different here is that most of the support seems to be for the bereaved spouse or for young children. Older children, grandchildren, siblings and friends don't usually get the attention and certainly not the understanding that the others get.

And if the bereaved community as a whole is underserved and poorly understood, these other, seemingly, although not really, peripheral members of the population get much less attention and understanding. We often don't know the depth of the connection between them and the person who has passed, and so it's very hard to gauge how, and how intensely, these other people are grieving. Also, the "don't show your grief" energy we've discussed in other places is even more powerful I think once the grief expands beyond the spouse and young child level.

So what can we do for them, especially early on when we are so deeply grieving and struggling so hard just to deal with our own pain and sadness? I know I didn't address my children's and grandchildren's grief much during my own earliest grief. I did talk to each of them later on as much as they were comfortable doing. As you might expect, I found different levels and different expressions of grief in each of them.

I really don't think I could have done much more in the depths of my grief because it so overwhelmed me. Because they all lived in Florida and weren't part of my daily life, I couldn't see it clearly and any needs they had weren't there for me to see every day.

If you are aware of their grief, especially young children living with you, it would be good to try to find ways to talk with them so they can express how they are feeling and how they are dealing with it. If you or they need to, this might also be a good time to find some family counseling or a support group for children and young adults.

In an aside about how this can move out away from us, I learned that not only was I mostly unaware of the effects of the grief my family felt for Andi, but I also was unaware of the effect my grieving had on others as well.

I recently had a conversation with my granddaughter Breana about something that surprised me. It's related to how grief effects others in our families and of how expressing our grief in front of family and children/grandchildren may effect them in particular. There is more on expressing grief in front of others in Chapter 11.

Bre had moved to Colorado and had been staying with me for about 3 months during the early part of my grief journey. As I've written before, I was very much expressing my grief when and where it came over me at that time, and so she saw me at a very raw time in my journey. At eighteen or nineteen years old, she saw and heard me break down in tears and sobbing grief on more than a few occasions.

I never considered what that might have looked like to her at the time, I was honestly way too overwhelmed by my grief to even think about it. She moved out of the area for college about a year later and I didn't get much chance to talk to her for a few years. She is now twenty four and has moved close by again. We recently had a very interesting conversation that included what she took away from that time and about how seeing me in so much pain made her feel.

Her take away was basically that she never wanted to get as close to someone as I had been to Andi because she never wanted to experience the kind of pain she was seeing me go through in my grief.

Whoa, that stopped my in my tracks!

My instant reaction however, was to tell her that I would never have traded one moment of my life with Andi nor any part of the love we shared to have avoided any of the pain of my grief. Every moment of our love was so much more important to us both than avoiding grief would or could ever have been for me, even if I had been able to imagine the grief before it happened.

Once I told her that, she said "Poppy, you have to put that in your book. It's one of the most important things you can tell people."

So here it is. While everyone gets to choose how and when they express their grief, I hope that if you do express it in front of others, that this story can remind you to somehow let children of any age know that love is always worth it. Love is not to be avoided to avoid grief. Love may be why we grieve, but it's the love that is the center of everything we were and did throughout our lives together. It is the reason for it all. And it is always worth it!

❀

Using Intent Statements to Chart our Paths. Choosing Intent Rather than Resolutions:

Since this chapter is mostly about holidays, I thought I would include an idea that I learned at a support group meeting I attended that has proven to be a very important part of my journey and growth. It's also something I do with all the support groups I now facilitate. It is something I still personally do at the beginning of each year to help me define an overall meaning and purpose for the year to come.

New Years resolutions are a tradition and breaking them is also a tradition. The idea of a resolution is pretty linear, it says "I will do this". It's pretty easy to make a resolution. It's also just as easy to break it, just don't do it and once you don't do it, you've broken it and it's done.

You can try to go back and revisit it, but you've already shown that it's not that important to not break it. You've probably said "I can always go back to it" but often that happens sporadically or not at all, we move on and leave the resolution behind. In a way, we have made and broken a promise to ourself and in another way it's a small (or not so small) failure. We didn't get it done! It's usually not terribly healthy to set ourselves up for failure...especially during the uncertainties of our grieving.

An intent is more non-linear. Intent is about how you want to live your life and focus your activities and thoughts for some period of time.

When we intend to do something, it is not so much a requirement as it is a plan. It defines a path and a direction and a movement that can come and go. It can be very forward and powerful or it can sit in the background; but the intent is always there to guide our thoughts and actions when we want or need it to.

Our New Years intent can be our blueprint for the year to come, more of a goal to move towards than a task to be completed. Little steps and small changes are just as important as large ones. Everything positive we do leads us towards healing and wellness.

Intent can help you to find meaning and direction in your life and give you a focus for growth that seems to me to be more gentle than a resolution.

Your intent can be whatever you want it to be. It can definitely be your guide and help you to focus on finding hope and healing and letting them grow to become wellness within you.

Your intent statement is something you can work on every day. You can say it out loud, think it in your head and/or make it part of a ritual or routine you follow. You can make it something you work on often throughout the year and in small steps, gradually see yourself become that intent as what you intend begins to manifest in your life.

Setting goals and expectations for ourselves for the new year:

So, this year, you might consider finding some goal and some expectation for the new year and define it by your intent statement. You can let it be your guide throughout the year ahead to help you find hope and healing and to embrace your grief and your opportunities to become more.

No matter when in the year you read this, as the next new year approaches, consider thinking about what you might intend to do and work on for the year ahead. Then write an intent statement for the new year instead of making resolutions.

I want to end this chapter by saying that for myself, when I've looked back on it at the end of each year, it was pretty clear that the prior year's intent statement had indeed set the tone and direction that my growth took during that year.

As an example of how it worked for me, during my period of learning to regain my self confidence, the intent statement I set for that year was "I am, I can and I will!" Every time I found myself thinking I can't in any way, I repeated that intent statement like a mantra. I repeatedly said in my head, "I am-I can-I will!" over and over, to remind myself to not be bound by illusions created by my grief, to not be bound by inertia and to not allow myself to be less but to continue to grow and be more.

I think the fact that this book got written and published out of the depths of my grief is a pretty good example of how well the process can and continues to work.

Some questions to consider :

• What are your feelings about experiencing your first of any of these days if you have not reached that point or how did you feel if you are past that point.?

• How does the anticipation of one of these days impact you? If you've been through them, was the actual event more or less difficult than the anticipation of them?

• Do (did) you want to avoid dealing with them the first time or would you rather meet them head-on or do some of both (struggle or surrender) ?

• During your year of firsts if you've had one, what turned out to be the most difficult day for you? Why?

- Do you want to hold on to old traditions, break old traditions, make new traditions, do nothing at all? Would you rather it changed each year and adapt what you do to each season and holiday to fill your changing needs and wants?

- How can you also respect and possibly meet the needs of others of your family and friends who may be very strongly grief-filled as well. What if their needs are different than yours? Can you, should you, will you compromise?

- Do you have any guilt about wanting to change things or from actually making changes? If so, how will you or are you dealing with it?

Chapter 6

Two Back-Stories

I want to add two back-stories here that I thought would help the flow of the book and perhaps help your understanding of what I experienced as well as a bit of the chronology of how things progressed for me.

The Music Story:

This is the back-story of the music that runs through my entire grief journey and through this entire book. It is also part of how I was able to come to recognize the spirit connection Andi and I still shared. It was a major part of what I saw and learned that helped me to "suspend my disbelief" and accept the continuing connection and communication that was happening between us. Looking back, it seems like it all took a very long time to unfold, but much of it actually happened during the first two years of my grief journey.

As with the Vision Story that follows, I thought it would be interesting and helpful to read it all together in one place and that it would also be helpful for me to see it and recall it as it unfolded if I could.

As background for this story, I have played guitar most of my life. I know I've written it before but Andi was an intuitive keyboard player. With no formal training, she could still sit and improvise for hours. She also wrote poems and verses and had some of her work published as greeting cards and in anthologies for Blue Mountain Arts.

Our first music adventure together was in 2004. I was playing with an Irish Pub Band at the time and Andi wrote a lovely song based on a trip we had taken to Ireland a few years earlier and I set it to a traditional Irish tune. The band ended up performing it regularly once it was completed.

That same year, Andi wrote a poem/song for me and I did the music again and it turned out to be a love song I still sing today.

It wasn't long after that song was written that Andi's cancer journey began. As we turned our attention in that direction, doing that song was unfortunately the last time we had the focus to create music together.

Fast forward to 2016.

I had begun to play the guitar every night in response to my encounter with the music counselor that I've written about in Chapter 14. As my playing evolved, I started trying to write songs but didn't have much luck until one day, as I was working with some chord progressions I had known for a while, words started coming to me. I got out a pad and pen and started writing them down and they eventually turned into a song about my grief.

I wrote a second song beginning in November of 2016 after a visit to see my brother in Oregon. During a day at the beach on the Oregon coast, I got another set of words coming into my head and when I got home I begin writing another song about waves of grief.

My granddaughter Khari called me at the end of 2016 to tell me she was getting married (smile). She knew I had been playing guitar and writing songs during my grief journey and she said, "Poppy, will you write me a song for my wedding?" No pressure there! I had been bereaved for around six months at that time and so I was still very heavily grieving. But how could a grandfather say no to that request? So I told her I would try.

Here's where it got interesting and I began to realize and understand, if not totally believe, that it wasn't totally me writing those songs. When I started working on the song for Khari, I had figured out some chords I wanted to use and as I was sitting playing, all of a sudden, I got a rush of words. I started writing as fast as I could, trying to capture them because I suddenly knew clearly that they were from Andi. She had sent them to me for Khari and the entire song came to me complete, as fast as I could write it down.

It took until April of 2017 to get it cleaned up, learned and recorded but I was able to bring Khari her Beba's words and my music, to surprise her and have them at the wedding reception and for she and I to dance together, tears flowing down both our faces as the DJ played the song! And I got to tell everyone at the reception how the song came into being…

There were more songs after that and with each one, I began to see more clearly and believe more deeply that they were indeed gifts from Andi (I can't write like that) and that she was often reaching deep within my emotions and showing me places I wasn't even aware of. The songs contained lessons and her deep love reaching out to me.

Those songs became guides throughout my grief journey. Even now, when I sing them, I not only hear Andi's voice but I sometimes learn something else, a new meaning and a new understanding comes to me that she put there for me to find when the time was right for me to hear them.

More love across the veil and the early parts of a creative sharing that has become more and more amazing as time goes on.

I always wanted Andi and I to be able to share our creative energy and do projects together. That led us at one point to her writing verses for me to put on photo images I had taken. We created Silver Dream Studio together to be the platform from which our creative sharing could reach out to the world.

We struggled sometimes to share what was basically our individual creative spaces. There is always a "mine" associated with creativity I think, that can be very hard to let go of and true creative sharing is always a difficult thing to achieve. We managed to do it sometimes and other times we argued over it but I still have a large number of things Andi wrote to grace my images that I treasure and try to share when and where I can.

With half a dozen songs written over about five years, we opened the next chapter of the sharing and the music journey. I've written in chapter 3 about the MIDI music and how Andi allowed me to be her instrument and bring her beautiful melodies back into the material world.

And then, with the ending of my grief journey, we wrote another song together in 2022 that for the first time was not necessarily about my grief. It is a song of grief but it was written for anyone who has experienced the silence in an empty, grief-filled home. But it's tone is different, it's not entirely about me anymore, it's a gift of something I've learned and Andi was able to put in words. I was able to put it to music that we can share with others as we shared the creative process of writing it.

And yet again, a surprise. I was sitting on the couch waiting for a friend to come to the house for dinner and I started thinking about some mantra-like phrases that had come into my head over the week or two before that night. For some reason I opened a new document on my computer and wrote one of them down. And then, again, Andi took over the writing, and words started flowing and kept coming until it contained almost everything I have learned on my spirit journey. All the lessons about being present in my life and letting spirit guide me intuitively were in there too. As with the wedding song, it came through whole and I've changed only the very smallest parts to help set the words to music.

The music, ahhh, the music. I thought since I couldn't find any chords in my head that I wanted to use or that I thought would go well with those words, that maybe we could create it on the MIDI keyboard. Maybe Andi would send her music that way too. But the next day, just to see what happened, I picked up the guitar and had the words in front of me and started to play and chords came to me that I hadn't played before in that way, or in those combinations. But they were resonating with the words so I spent the entire day just sitting there playing, doing one line at a time, one verse at a time, working and reworking each part of it and building the song as each piece came together and fell into place. It was essentially complete in three days.

Amazing!

✿

The Vision Story(s):

I'm going to tell a story here about connections and confluences and how intent and spirit brought things into my life during my grief journey. I've put it together with the music story in this chapter because they are connected. While this story touches on a number of things that I've written about in other places, this is more about the flow of how they came together and unfolded during my grief journey as I learned them. It's also about how they influenced my life and the role they played in my healing journey.

As I keep reminding you, this is just what happened to me. I don't know if anyone else will experience anything like this, but I do know that intent and finding meaning and purpose in our lives, however we experience and create them, are very important parts of the healing journey.

I think the beginning of this story came with a song I began to work on in October of 2019. I started playing around with some chords on the guitar and all of a sudden, as I described in the music story, I got a wave of words filling me that had Andi's flavor to them. I started writing them down as quickly as I could to capture what she was sending me.

The entire first draft came in a rush, in only 15 minutes or so. When the words stopped flowing, I set about putting the words to the music of the chords I had been playing. It was a fairly complex song so it kept morphing and being refined bit by bit all through the rest of the year as I made the changes it needed to make it feel right.

It was the beginning of something large and important that I didn't really recognize at the time. I was just thrilled to have gotten the gift of the words from Andi and the engagement of my attention for so long in crafting it into the song that it became.

Here's the chorus as it ended up and it seems to me to be a pretty strong indication of what was happening in my mind and emotions at that time. The song captured and exposed feelings I didn't know I had within me and clearly showed me that I was needing a meaning and purpose in my life fairly strongly. There is also a strong element of hope in it as well:

I'm looking for a phoenix moment,
looking outward towards the sun,
looking just to rise up singing,
one more time before I'm done…

From Phoenix Moment (© Andi and Howard Fischer, 2019)

Now to the rest of the story and how it all ties together…

I've written about intent statements in Chapter 5 and how they can be a powerful force for focusing our thinking and growth. This part of the story begins in late 2019 and my intent statement for that year had been: I am, I can and I will. It was about learning to recover my self confidence and overcoming inertia and it had as a secondary layer, as the song suggests, the rebuilding of the meaning and purpose in my life that had been shattered and destroyed in my grief.

Throughout the year, one of the things that I had been working on a lot was exploring what I thought was important in my (new) life. I needed to find what I could become and what I could dedicate myself to that would give me a reason to go on. Again, looking back, it all turned out to be reflected in the song.

The first thought that resonated with me as I looked for that meaning and purpose was to do whatever it was I chose to do in honor of Andi and in her name, to keep who she was clear and strong in both my memories and in my interactions, to honor her with everything I did, and to allow her to still be an influence in the world through my actions.

Throughout the rest of the year, once that initial idea was in place, I gradually came to see that what I was getting the most healing from and some good feelings from as well, was the work I was doing organizing the potlucks and social activities for the group of bereaved spouses and partners I was involved with. It was still fairly basic then, mostly a monthly potluck and perhaps one evening a month going to a wine bar for conversation. I've expanded the story of how that worked and how that part of my journey evolved in Chapter 11.

Sometime in November of that year, I had a major vision. It came to me and I'm sure now that it came from Andi, that I should dedicate myself and my life to hope and healing. That I should build a life based on helping the community of bereaved spouses and partners I was coming to know, and to see if there were ways I could do even more to help share what I was learning. Could I help bring people together for them to begin to build new lives with others who shared a similar journey and need?

At that point I didn't really know how it was going to happen but in a confluence that occurred in the weeks that followed, I had an unexpected conversation with a friend in my support group. She told me that she was volunteering at the Community Grief Center in Greeley and that they didn't have any support there for bereaved spouses. She suggested I get in touch with the director and see if there was anything I could do there to help. It took a few weeks for me to decide to move on the suggestion but I ended up setting up an appointment to visit with Dr. Debby Baker, the director of the grief center.

I met with Dr. Baker and as we were talking, I told her that I would love to be able to do some support work; to do something to help bereaved spouses and partners. I told her that I was willing to volunteer to do some kind of class or meeting. I was thinking of maybe a lecture-type get together to talk about things I had learned and experienced, no doubt based on my teaching experience.

As we continued to talk, she suggested that I might think about doing a support group meeting once a month and amazingly, she said that she trusted my intentions and background and what I had learned about grief. She said I could do it however I wanted, and that I could create it and present it for anyone who wanted to join us for the meetings.

I was overwhelmed and honored. I guess I also needed someone to affirm and trust that I was capable of doing something like that to help me believe it myself at that time. It was the perfect thing just then to help me in the process of recovering my self confidence. It was just what I needed to hear and I very gratefully said I would do it and I thought we could start in January for the first meeting.

And then I went home and freaked out. I had just committed to doing something huge! And I realized that oh, now I really was going to have to overcome inertia and actually write the things I wanted to talk about, build the topics and meeting notes, and basically start to create it all from scratch. And then I had to actually make it happen!

It was definitely a double-edged sword. It was exactly what I wanted and needed, it used all my skills and what I had learned about bereavement, but it was going to be a lot of work and a responsibility that I was not going to be able to avoid. I was going to have to do the work, and make it work not just for myself, but for all the people I thought might come and be part of the group.

But wow, it so neatly fit into my intent and the growth of my new meaning and purpose. And I really was honored and grateful that someone thought that I might have something to give that would be helpful and worthwhile. It was a major gift I was being given that I knew would be a serious aid to my self confidence if I could overcome the inertia and actually make it happen. Of course it would be pretty nasty if I couldn't make it happen but in a way, I left myself no choice. I said I would and I needed to do it for both myself and for Andi.

So I spent hours almost everyday for the rest of the year thinking about topics and a general idea of what I would say or do in a meeting. Then I "worked my butt off" writing the first set of notes and lecture materials and handouts. I was still thinking like a college professor but more importantly, I was thinking... and growing and moving forward and building something new that I could give as a gift in Andi's honor.

As the New Year turned to 2020, it was time to set my new intention for the coming year and for 2020, in response to all the work I had been doing, the intent statement I chose was: To promote and be hope and healing!

I decided to do all I could to help and support the bereaved community I now had access to and build what I could to aid them in creating hope and healing in their lives using what I had learned and was still learning about how to create it in my own life. I also learned, as time went by, that my taking on this task and responsibility was a very important part of my own growth towards healing and wellness.

We had the first three meetings of the Hope and Healing Widow and Widowers Support Group at the beginning of 2020 and then COVID shut everything down. Everything went on hold but I decided to keep writing and putting new topics together for when we came back together. I even did something very difficult for me at the time, I went into my grief journal and read everything I had written and documented during the first year of my bereavement so I could use it as it had actually unfolded for me in creating my notes. Very valuable to do but it sure generated lots of tears!

Once the support group began to meet again, Andi sent me another vision. Perhaps I could share what I was writing and presenting at the support group meetings with a larger group of people. Perhaps I could build a web page or something like that and post it online for people to find.

I told my daughter about that idea and she said "why don't you do a blog Dad." I didn't even know what a blog was at that time.

So we had some conversations, I looked at a bunch of stuff online and in the end found a template for a blog. With my daughter's help, I began to create it, to post notes from the meetings and even to include a number of the photos and graphics Andi and I had done together over the years. The blog is still at wavesofgrief2020.org.

And amazingly yet again, there was another confluence that opened yet another door which turned out to be a major part of the evolution of the spirit connection Andi and I were finding and building. As I was working on photo's for the blog, Andi started sending me new words and short verses to add to my images so we could do them together again and I was able to bring her words into the world again in yet another way.

And then I got COVID. Just a mild case compared to what I was hearing people were experiencing around the world, but even at that, I was ill for months. I also was isolated by the general shut down that happened just then and pretty much went through a return of my early grief and the powerful inertia it contained. I also lost a large amount of my physical energy and for a time I thought I would not recover it and would have to move to be close to my daughter so that she could take care of me.

Fortunately, that didn't happen and although it took almost two years, I did finally recover all of my energy and my thinking became more clear again. Also, when the restrictions ended, I was able to go back to facilitating the support group meetings and carrying on where we had left off.

One more vision came to me after that. After a year or so, I had written so much and posted so much on the blog that Andi showed me that what I needed to do ultimately was to combine all the blog notes, all the support group notes, and lots of stories from my grief journey into a book and publish it. It seemed like such a perfect next step at the time that I dedicated myself to doing it. I promised to myself and to Andi that I would somehow make it happen. It took over two years to come to completion but here it is!

So it all just happened as it happened. I really didn't plan it or choose any of it, it just unfolded for me, perhaps as a result of the intent I had set and kept to each year and also through Andi's love. Looking back, I am amazed not so much that the visions happened but that somehow in the midst of my grieving, I was able to tap into such a huge amount of positive and creative energy and overcome my inertia to actualize it.

It ultimately helped me to create a new meaning and purpose in my life that honored Andi. In the end, having the visions and the doing of it helped me to find my way to hope, healing and wellness.

And as a last note to finish the story, I have to add that all of this proved to be the final piece in "suspending my disbelief" and coming to fully accept that Andi was still present in my life in spirit and that we had been given the gift of continuing our love, perhaps to allow me to learn to help others, to share my journey as I could and to honor Andi as I did it.

My intent led me true; I did indeed become hope and healing and build a new meaning and purpose in my life that I continue to hold and follow today.

Learning to Live Again and Reconstruction

Chapter 7

Seeking Understanding, Meaning and Purpose

S *ome things to think about that we may feel and not understand:*

You're not going crazy, everything is ok to think and feel but not necessarily to act upon.

Many of the things going through our minds during our grieving, especially in our early grief, may have us doubting our sanity at times. They may be so outside our normal experiences and ways of thinking and acting that we wonder if we have "lost it" and if we will ever be able to function or think clearly or "normally" again. Most of these things are direct effects of our grief and the good thing is, like the waves of grief and the pain and sadness, they tend to become less common and less severe over time.

With that said, please remember the negative places I've written about and turn away from them. Don't get stuck dwelling on them and please don't embrace or act on them even if they do come into your mind. Just because you think of something, that doesn't make it something you have to do or even accept or believe. Please remember to find help to do so if you can't get past them on your own.

The Piñata effect: An image...

When we experience the passing of a spouse or partner, our entire world is disrupted, all we know and all we have been is shaken to its very core and all we were is shattered and thrown to the winds. Our thoughts travel to places we may never have been before, we doubt many of our sure of's, and everything becomes distorted from what we are used to.

While we may sometimes feel like we are "going crazy," it's probably because we are likely experiencing a total disorientation and distortion of everything in our lives. In many ways, it's like a form of PTSD (Post Traumatic Stress Disorder) and since what is happening to us is a fairly common reaction to our grief, maybe it's just PTS, and not a disorder at all.

This next idea reflects how I thought about a group of those disconnected and disoriented thoughts and feelings when I was experiencing them. To help me understand them, I called it the Piñata Effect when it was happening to me.

Think of a piñata, that's our minds, the stick we strike it with is our grief. A stick strikes the piñata (our minds) in the moment of our loss and everything inside, like the things inside the piñata, tumbles out of place, maybe to the ground. If you pick it all up off of the ground and try to put it back inside the piñata in its original place, it probably won't go back the way it came out and things will get jumbled and twisted and some may not go back in at all.

In our minds, after things "tumble out" during our earliest and heaviest grief, we may not even recognize what is going on or even what is happening to us, because it's all so different now. Things are in a different order, they are often not familiar to us and our normal thinking processes are disrupted and unrecognizable. The "fog" sets in. So it's not surprising we can be confused or disoriented or sometimes unable to do even simple tasks until we find ways to reorder and realign our thoughts and feelings in a new way to accommodate what has happened in our minds and our lives.

I've also wondered if grief could also be like an "emotional stroke" where our thinking and emotions and feelings are disconnected from their normal pathways by the trauma and pain we have experienced. As with a physical stroke, we are, in a sense, debilitated for a time until we are able to retrain ourselves and find new pathways for our thoughts and emotions to accommodate and facilitate the changes and the new ways of thinking and feeling that our grief has brought us to.

Having a phoenix moment:

As we move further into our journeys and reach a place in our grieving when we have some control over what our lives look like, we may also reach a place where we decide to move forward and start to build and grow our new lives intentionally and constructively. Partially because of the song we wrote, I have been calling that time of choice a "phoenix moment."

Whenever we reach it in our journey, it's a place where we can make the choice to begin to move forward with intent. It's a time when we can begin to rise out of the ashes of our grief and begin to create our new lives, to choose who we are going to become, who we are going to travel with, and begin to forge a new meaning and purpose that will guide us as we move forward.

Sometimes the phoenix moment can come unexpectedly and be like an Aha! moment that happens kind of organically and just appears in our lives. Other times, it's more consciously directed, and done because we feel it's time to take more control of our lives and begin to move forward. Either way, it represents a point of change in our grief and healing journeys, perhaps it's the time when our healing journey begins to overtake our grieving and starts to become dominant. It can mark the start of reconstructing our lives.

❀

The Beginnings of Reconstruction:

Reconstruction is the term I use to talk about building foundations for the future and the new life we will have ahead of us. The constructive things you do, in the early months especially, I found, can set the stage and give you a strong base on which to build during the healing processes to come. Your approach to healing can play a large role in how your grief journey, your healing journey and your bereavement as a whole progresses as you start to reconstruct your life.

When I asked for some thoughts on reconstruction from members of a support group, Tom, one of our facilitators wrote, partially from things he had read and partially from his own experience:

"Grief keeps pulling our thoughts back to the shared memories and the lost future that we had with our spouse. Dreaming and planning for your future is an important part of what makes us human. It gives us hope that tomorrow, or next year, will be better, that we will continue to gain life experiences and memories together. When a spouse dies, that shared future dies as well. And, without that, part of us dies too. Building a new future is important to our emotional well being; and, critical to our recovery (healing) from grief."

As I personally moved forward, something I often asked myself, near the beginning and later in the journey as well, was, can I find a way to use my grief and the reconstruction that accompanies it in a positive way to grow and become more?

I believe that the next two ideas may be among the most important things I learned and did to promote my healthy journey to healing and wellness.

Finding meaning and purpose as we start to restructure our lives:

A loss of meaning and purpose is something most spouses and partners experience as a large part of their grief. At some level our spouse or partner and our love for each other were central to all the meaning and purpose we had in our relationship and in our lives.

Since our shared meaning and purpose has been taken from us, as part of the healing process we now need to redefine the purpose and meaning in our lives for ourselves alone. We now need to learn how to create and use a new purpose and meaning to guide us, to help fill the empty places, and to give us ways and reasons to go forward in our lives.

Finding meaning and purpose in our new lives can (and maybe should) become a "full time job."

It took a while, towards the end of my first year actually, before it became clear that meaning and purpose were missing in my life and that I needed to redefine these things for myself. It took longer before I figured out ways and patterns of thinking that allowed me to begin that process and to start to find a new reason to live and thrive within my still fragile grief journey.

I was at a yoga class one day and the teacher asked us to choose an intent for the session, something to guide our meditation and to bring our thoughts back to if they wandered throughout the hour. She asked us to make that intent a first person and present thought, not an I want to do or be something, but an I am something type of thought.

I had already begun to feel, through the support groups and social group I was helping to bring together, that it would be important to my growth and also to honor Andi, to devote my time and myself to helping others in the bereavement community where I lived. As is probably evident throughout my writings, I used the phrase "creating hope and healing" often to describe what I was trying to do, both for myself and for others.

So my intent that day started as "I want to be hope and healing" and then more clearly in the way we were asked to do it, it changed to "I am hope and healing." It was a very transformative moment for me. By the end of the session, I had been repeating "I am Hope and Healing" many times, over and over in my mind.

It felt very right to me at the time to take that forward and make that intent a part of what I did and to come to believe it was indeed who and what I was. As I embraced that in thought, it shaped my life and my grief and healing journeys.

All of what I did for the next four years within the reconstruction of my new life was in some way built on that intent. So many things evolved and came into being as part of that intent. Through it, I began building the social group structure in my community and eventually creating and leading the support group for bereaved spouses and partners in Greeley. The blog I created and this book are direct outgrowths of that intent as well.

The important part of the story is how much active work and time I spent on building a new life full of new meaning and purpose. The learning to live again it contained and the learning to become more it required of me, carried me and helped shape my grief journey from actively grieving to healing and eventually to wellness. It was also a way for me to honor Andi in all I did and all I became. All that I did in that context became a gift to honor her.

As always, this is just my story and everyone gets to find and move though their own grief and reconstruction in their own way and create their own stories. But the commonality that I want to stress here is that finding a new meaning and purpose can be of major importance in our healing and in shaping how we move forward and learn to live again. It is, I believe, central to our movement through our healing journey and to our finding wellness within and beyond our grief.

✿

Honoring our loved ones as we define and create the new purpose and meaning in our lives:

As we begin our reconstruction, how can we allow our "new" lives to still contain our love and our connections with our loved ones? How can we allow our new lives to reflect and honor our spouses or partners? Can we choose to do things and become more of the person they would have approved or affirmed us becoming?

Can we change things about ourselves or become better at things we already are? Can we do these things in their honor and as a gift to them and to ourselves, believing that we will become better for our efforts?

If, in the often deep examination of ourselves, our lives and our memories that grief often brings, we find things we could have or should have done differently or better, perhaps what we can do now is to learn from them and make peace with them as done and unchangeable. In our evaluation of those things, if we feel we need to, we can perhaps change behaviors that need changing and do so in a way that honors our loved ones by us becoming better now. Perhaps we can apologize to them in our minds and from our hearts and spirits for things we might regret.

These changes in ourselves that I'm referring to are things we may not have had time to do or the will to do in the middle of our everyday lives. In our bereavement, we have a lot of time to fill and that time can now be available for us to learn, change and grow in. Choosing to do these things in a direction our spouses or partners would have loved for us to do is a very powerful way to honor them and to make our memories and our love even stronger and more a part of who we are.

We can even allow them to forgive us if forgiveness is needed and we can forgive ourselves as well. We can learn, change if we need to, and then use those changes as a way to aid us as we look for ways to move forward.

No matter how long my journey goes on, sometimes I still remember something from our life that I might have done better, something I might have said or not said or something I should have been aware of that slipped by me during our time together. When I do, I try to stop and apologize to Andi and let her know I now see more clearly something that happened or was said or something I wish I had been better at during that moment in the past.

Then, because I can't change the past, I don't allow myself to dwell on it, I instead try to change those behaviors I can change. In her honor, I try to see more clearly and behave more like what she would have wanted me to. I believe it helps both of us for me to do this.

For me, it is also very important to be committed to actually making the changes and not just having the thoughts. Not just asking for forgiveness but doing what needs to be done to deserve it.

So, as we begin to build our new lives, and work to find new meaning and purpose, we can also let it be an opportunity to honor our spouses and partners if we choose to, and try to incorporate things they would have wanted us to be and do in what we choose to do going forward.

What would they want us to do? How would they want us to behave? How can what we now choose to do honor them and help us hold their memories in our hearts, minds and actions?

A caution about how we think about the past and things we did or didn't do:

Dwelling on the past and things we cannot change or undo does nothing constructive that I can see. It can often be a very destructive mental behavior that our grief can sometimes lead us to and keep us doing. We may benefit from thinking about those things from the past, of finding out how we feel about them now, but thinking about things is not the same as dwelling on them.

Thinking about them is very different from letting thoughts repeat without resolution over and over or becoming caught in a mental loop of frustration and guilt going round and round, that keeps us from healing and may actually move us away from healthy thinking and healing.

Not that it doesn't happen. Not that we don't all do these things from time to time, and not just during our grief. But coming to accept the things we can't change about the past is an important part of finding any kind of emotional healing and reaching a place of wellness.

Maybe grief is "normal" and so is healing:

Here's something to think about to wrap up this chapter. Since grief arises out of love, and since love is normal, maybe so is grief. Maybe grief is something we need to go through; something we need to acknowledge and embrace even though it's painful. Gradually, however, it will transform into healing and as we move through our grief, we open the door to a new life beyond the pain, transforming our memories and our love to allow us to go forward. People have been doing both for all of human history, so we can too.

Some Questions:

- *Have you felt a loss of meaning and purpose in your life?*

- *Does the lack of meaning and purpose make it hard to find reasons to do things?*

- *Do you think that the loss of meaning and purpose is significant in keeping you from wanting to move forward in your life?*

- *Can you begin to think of ways to create new meaning and purpose?*

- *What might you do to help you find them?*

- *Can you think of ways to honor your loved one in the ways you choose to move forward and seek meaning and purpose?*

Chapter 8

Dealing with the Material world -
Life goes on!

In the earliest parts of our grief journeys, when almost everything seems impossible, there are still things that unfortunately have to be done to get us through the days. Very early, we have to find ways to get through the funeral/memorial and perhaps the internment. We need to navigate all the financial and business types of things that still continue, even though in our minds, our lives seem to have stopped. We may still have to go to work and function or try to function every day.

Although we can be immobilized by our early grief, there are things that not only need to be done, but most times, it's our responsibility to do them. Finding our way through this seeming contradiction is one of the very hardest of the early lessons we have to learn and I believe that we all have to find our own way to do it.

Some suggestions and thoughts:

Allowing people to help you is usually a good thing. Being as strong as you can be and doing as much as you can do is good also. But when it becomes overwhelming, if there are people you trust available to share the work and help you to keep your focus and your strength, it's ok to do that for as long and as much as is helpful. Seeking professional help and being part of a support group are also very positive ways to "dilute" the burden we are shouldering, especially early on.

You probably can't turn all your affairs over entirely, and it's important to try to not let other people make decisions for you that you need to make for yourself, but help is always good if it's available. If it's not, then time can be your friend. Sometimes you just have to hold on, go forward when you can, take breaks when you need to, let your grief wash over you when it does, and then pick yourself up and go at it again.

Going back to work if you have to is always a challenge. I don't think we ever get enough time to grieve, to get through the most intense parts of our grieving before we are expected to be back doing what we have always done and perhaps to face the "get over it" energy of other people's expectations.

People at work, and in most other places too, often don't understand or know how or what to say or do and it can be painful or even hurtful when they say or do things that seem insensitive to you at the time. Mostly, I suspect that they are probably trying to be kind and helpful but really don't know how and so some of it may come across badly. More on this later…

A difficult part of going back to work seems to be finding the focus to do your job, to think clearly, to do the tasks in front of you and sometimes even to remember what you did 20 minutes ago. It's often a challenge to be able to interact without crying or to go through a meeting and actually know what was said or know what you needed to say.

It's not just at work that we face these things. Pretty much anything that needs focus is a challenge since focus is one of the things we have the least of at this time. I believe it's ok to give yourself permission to take a "grief moment" and step away when you need to and then come back to the task or meeting or whatever and go forward again.

Some people may not understand, but it's your grief and you have the right to express it as you need to and in some ways fit the other parts of your life around your grieving rather than fitting your grieving into the other parts of your life.

How do we talk to and deal with the professionals, trades people and others who we need to deal with? How do we make decisions about arrangements that may or may not have been made in advance?

Again, help from trusted friends and family can help us get through many of these things but in the end, it helps to find a way to do it or have it done as close to our own way as possible. If we can, it's also usually better if it is done in our own time and in what ever order and whatever way we can find to get it done. Difficult as it is, I believe it's important to be as careful and aware as you can be if you turn things over to someone who may then do it their way and not yours.

I talked to someone about this subject and they were very newly bereaved and still in "shock" from what had happened but they were also responsible for putting on and attending a child's wedding. The main comments I took away from the conversation that apply here include first, that it was pretty confusing having extreme sadness on one hand and the joy of the wedding on the other.

Also, they told me that the entire event was done in a fog but their grief was put aside so that what had to be done got done. The importance of making the wedding a happy and special event overrode the grief for that period of time but once everyone left and the needs of the wedding were done, the person I talked to knew it was going to "hit me hard" and the grieving process was going to take over.

This is something I've heard in other versions and situations and I have a favorite quote from Andi that seems to encapsulate the feelings and our ability to do what needs to be done.

"You never know how strong your are until you need to be."

Yet again, it's your life and your grief and everything should get as much input from you with as much strength as you can give it. I do think it is good to try to do as much as you feel you need to and are able to, pretty much everywhere along the way.

Do what you can, do what you must and if you do turn things over to others, try to let them do it. Try not to find fault if it is reasonably different from how you might have done it if you had been able to as long as the task gets done. If how they want to do something is so widely divergent from how you would have done it and you really don't like how or what someone is doing for you or in your name, I believe it's ok to ask them to step back or stop and return the task to you so it can be done more as you would wish it to be done.

❀

Caring for ourselves:

Some things and places that I think are important to pay attention to in our bereavement include sleeping and eating well, exercising, taking care of our bodies (and our immune systems) and keeping our physical surroundings relatively clean and safe. It's also important to be kind to ourselves as our grief and healing journeys cause us to look closely at ourselves as well as at our memories of our loved ones and things that happened in our lives together.

Our grief can make us sick. Especially early on, it can take our strength and our health and spiral them downhill. I, for example, lost 45 pounds and much of my physical strength durning the last six months of Andi's cancer journey and my early bereavement.

We are often so bereaved early on that we don't want to eat, we are sick feeling and the thought of food just doesn't sound very good. Cooking sounds even more difficult. We spend a lot of time sitting and not getting any exercise and maybe the most - besides the grief itself - debilitating part of early grief is not being able to sleep. All of these can drain away our health and even prolong our periods of intense grief because we lack any stamina to do anything other than sit and feel bad and "drown in our grief."

We all ultimately need to find ways to deal with these things. I have a brother-in-law who sent me a text every day starting after Andi's memorial to ask me if I was eating. He did that for months until he was sure that I had regained the will to start cooking and eating healthy meals again.

Thinking back, I believe that maybe beginning to be part of a group of bereaved spouses and partners who were having potlucks and making food to share was also a big help in getting me to eat and prepare meals again. The leftovers from the potlucks were always great to have and eat for a few days.

Also, if you've cooked before, learning how to cook for one is a problem you may face. It's hard to make smaller portions of old recipes and it can be sad cooking and eating them or trying to change them as well.

Learning to store food, to make your own "frozen dinners" is a way to avoid throwing stuff away, to avoid feeling like you are making too much or having to try to modify familiar recipes. It also gives you something to eat on days when you really don't want to cook. I bought a vacuum sealer to use for leftovers or to let me prepare large portions of meals to eat later and it has worked very well. It has become a major part of my kitchen tools and routines. There is always a meal in the freezer I can go to when I don't want to cook.

Being kind to ourselves is important too as our journey causes us to look closely at ourselves, our lives and our memories of our loved ones. It is more subtle than taking care of our physical needs but I think it's something we need to be aware of.

Re-thinking things we've done or said endlessly, looping imaginary conversations and revisiting or "beating ourselves up" about things in the past that we can't change are pretty common grief experiences. They can also be pretty counter-productive and they definitely aren't healing behaviors.

Being careful with medications and alcohol:

It's always a temptation to "drown our sorrow," to try to make the pain go away by medicating it in some way. We may also need something to help us fall asleep and stay asleep through the night or fall back asleep if we wake during the night. We may need something to help spark our appetite. We may even be prescribed medications for these things by our doctors. I don't believe it's necessarily bad to use some of these things to help ourselves, to dull the pain from time to time, to help us sleep when we can't stop thinking.

The danger I see and hear about is in over-using and becoming dependent on these things instead of using them as an aid. It's letting them become a crutch and allowing them to take over your grief and your life that becomes dangerous. If you know that you have addictive tendencies, I believe it is important for you to be especially careful about using any types of medications or alcohol for relief during your bereavement.

I personally found that a glass of wine with dinner or maybe later in the evening was relaxing and helped to take the edge off for a bit. CBD's seem to be a sleep aid and a mild anxiety reducer. And hey, I live in Colorado; occasionally smoking a little weed is always a possibility if it's legal and works for you. I've recently learned about some CBD/THC mixes that seem to focus on helping promote sleep that don't seem to have any "get you high" aspects to them that might be worth checking out if you live somewhere they are available legally.

I used that glass of wine at dinner and was taking prescription Ativan regularly through the first months of my grief. They both helped me relax and sleep so I found them to be useful. When my doctor told me Ativan could be addictive, it was time to find more benign ways of getting medication help.

I kept up the glass of wine but gradually stopped taking the Ativan and eventually started taking CBD's to help me sleep and take a bit of the anxiety out of my days. That turned out to be a much better solution. It also became one glass of wine or two on a special night. It was not to get drunk, stop thinking or feeling however, it was just to take some of the edginess away and because I like drinking nice wine with dinner.

After taking them for over a year, I've stopped using CBD's now too. They taught me how to fall asleep again and if I wake, I seem to be able to fall back asleep relatively quickly. My careful and intentional use of those gentle medications allowed me to re-train my body so it now seems to remember how to sleep normally.

To me, it appears that it's your reason and intent in doing any medications, alcohol or drugs that can change them from positive aids to negative influences and that it can happen without you realizing it. Especially with medications and recreational drugs, it can often happen before you know it. Please pay attention to your usage and don't rationalize "just one more time." I've been told that if you feel you have to instead of you want to, then that is a really good time to seriously reconsider what you are doing.

What is healthy and what is not:

Healthy implies things functioning relatively normally without an overwhelming number of negative events or things in our daily lives. It is also about things that we do that are positive and have a positive effect on us and in the same way, things that have negative effects on us are unhealthy.

Healthy behaviors, a very brief list:

- Taking care of ourselves both physically and mentally.
- Sleeping and eating well.
- Becoming active and taking on our responsibilities.
- Crying and letting our grief express itself in positive ways.
- Telling our stories.
- Seeking and accepting help when we feel overwhelmed.
- Carefully using medications, drugs or alcohol.
- Creating mental and emotional habits of healing.
- What ever works that you try or experience that has a positive effect goes here.

Unhealthy Behaviors, also a very brief list:

- Not sleeping well.
- Not eating well.
- Compulsive eating throughout the day.
- Not being active.
- Not doing things we are responsible for, including taking care of ourselves.
- Becoming isolated.
- Thinking about doing or actually doing harm to ourselves and/or others.
- Abusing medications, drugs or alcohol.
- Expressing uncontrolled anger.
- Negative thinking.
- Inappropriate behavior towards others.
- Letting our grief become habitual.
- Listening to and getting involved in other people's angry and negative comments about their grief and their grief journeys.
- Anything you do or experience that has a negative effect goes here.

Some positive things to consider doing:

Journaling: Chronicling our thoughts and our days, writing letters to our loved one; things we still want to say or new things we want to tell them now!

Journals can be a private place to explore your thoughts and feelings. They allow you to express things you don't want to share with anyone else but that you need to work on and find your way through as you navigate your grief journey. They can be a way to get thoughts out of your mind when you no longer have someone physically there with you to share them with. Journals can be hand written in a book or as a computer file, or whatever you are comfortable with.

Journaling at the end of the day can be a very healing tool. It was for me. It allowed me to write about and tell Andi about my day, about my feelings, about things I learned and thought and was always a place for memories. It helped me to remember things and it helped to get thoughts outside of my mind and into my e-journal.

Writing them allowed me to validate them but also to release them from building up inside me and clogging my mind and emotions with the often very heavy and ponderous thoughts and feelings that my grief brought me each day. I also used my journal to reinforce routines and rituals I tried or practiced during the day.

Journaling also allows us to write not only for and to ourselves. It's a place and a way to express thoughts and feelings we might want to share with our loved ones. We can write as if we are "talking" to them and as if they can "hear" what we write. It can be helpful and healing to let these thoughts and feelings move outside of our minds and take on the tangible reality of being readable on paper or a computer screen.

"Mindful stuff" like yoga and meditation, crafting or hobbies can help our focus and healing and help break the habits of grief and inertia. Walking can help soothe our grief and keep us moving.

Being present in your grief:

Sometimes grief can really be a pretty mindful state. Being mindful is just another way of saying that we are being fully present in each moment. It's like being totally focused on a task we are doing and not thinking about anything else while we are doing it.

While we think about or dwell on the past in our thoughts of our loved ones a lot during our grief, the waves of grief, the very emotional and visceral feelings of pain and loneliness that overtake us, are actually very present moments for us in the times when the pain and sense of loss they create in us take over. We are totally present in the pain we feel.

That is actually a very mindful place. It's not necessarily a peaceful place or a comfortable place but it is, in a way, a form of mindful meditation that can be a part of opening our minds to exploring who we are and how we are and allow us to work on ourselves. It's a time when that meditative place may give us an opportunity to figure out some things, like what to leave in and what to leave out from our old lives or what we want to change if we choose to as we create our new lives without our loved ones.

Grief is a journey not a destination:

Grief is ongoing but it also changes through time. We grieve through time and we experience our grief differently each day, sometimes in each moment. There isn't really a destination we are heading towards, grief is just a part of our lives, moment to moment. How it changes is partially a function of time but also of how we choose to experience our grief and work with it.

If we are not our grief, then grief is something we experience. Since we are already grieving, in a sense, grief is then also a journey towards healing and wellness, its not a destination we are heading for, we are already there, we are already grieving.

What happens day by day through time is the journey of your life. During our grief and healing journeys, keeping busy, learning new things, doing mundane things and filling the lonely time with tasks we enjoy are some of the things we can do to get through the time as it passes. It's the time passing, the doing, the journey, that is important though we may not notice it happening. It's what we do as we learn to live again.

We didn't choose the situations we find ourselves in. As circumstances happened in our lives, they moved us towards our grief with the passing of our loved ones.

Now, while it may feel like everything has stopped and frozen in place, time, life, and the world all continue as they always have and so we also continue to journey though our lives.

Being without our loved ones, we now journey seemingly alone and in some ways, we are without a map, blazing a trail and just experiencing each moment of the journey that is our lives, as we move forward. There is an element of mindfulness here as well.

During my early grief, I know I spent a lot of time being totally present as the immediacy of my pain and the feelings I was going through absorbed my attention completely, especially when the heaviest waves of grief overtook me. Much of the rest of the time when the waves were not rolling over me, I usually spent in the past, thinking about Andi, thinking about things we'd done and places we'd been as well as things we might have or wanted to have said or done in the future.

In general, the more present we can become moment to moment during our grief journeys, the more time we can spend not dwelling on our loss and on just trying to be calm and centered. The less time we spend thinking about and experiencing the pain and the things we no longer have and of all the sad and lonely times we are facing, the more we allow hope and healing to grow within us.

Finding something to do that is mindful or one pointed was a good way to take me out of my grief for a while and to give me a start on creating mental and emotional habits of healing and something other than grieving. By one pointed here, I mean being totally focused on a task or thought (like a mantra). I revisited old hobbies from earlier in my life and they gradually filled in a lot of time in my new life with something concentrated and one pointed to do that helped me a lot.

Walking is another very healthful process. Walking is good for your body, it keeps you moving and helps you build body strength and improves the functioning of your immune system.

Walking is also a good way, time and place to think outside your normal space and routines. It's a time to be out of doors and to see things in a new way perhaps. It frees your mind to wander, sometimes to grieve, sometimes to cry but also sometimes to think and look at your life and yourself. It can be a time to begin the work of deciding how you want to structure and create the next part of your life. It's an activity that can foster positive and healing thinking.

I spent as many hours walking as I possibly could, especially in the very early days. Since I had become so weak and unwell during the last six months or so of Andi's life and my early grief journey, it took me months to get myself physically strong enough and to have the stamina to walk two to three miles a day. Once I worked up to it and could do it, those walks and talking to Andi on them, were where I worked out most of what I learned about grief and about hope and healing. They are still part of most of my days as healing has grown into wellness and I've begun to actively live again.

Talking to your spouse or partner:

Another thing most of the bereaved spouses I talk to have at one time or another told me is that they often talk to their spouses when they are "alone" at home. There are so many parts of that to explore. First and most obviously, it fills some of the heavy silence that accompanies our being alone. It also lets us create rituals that bring us in contact with our loved ones, at least in thought, as we talk. It can create a feeling of continuity and in some ways let us feel less alone and it can build the feeling that perhaps they are not completely gone from our lives.

There is also the possibility that they may actually hear us to consider and the even more surprising possibility that they may answer in some way. I have written about these possibilities, including stories of some other things I have experienced in Chapter 3.

From a healing perspective, talking to our loved ones allows us to continue to do a very important part of what most of our lives with our loved ones contained. It lets us continue to tell them of our day and to let them be a sounding board for our ideas. It even allows us to let them continue to be the person we bitch to about stuff that happens in our lives. It can become a way to even ask them questions and use that to help us work our way through the possibilities and find answers to those questions that is often easier to do verbally than isolated in our minds.

I always find that it is easier to work though something when I talk it out to Andi then when I try to do it in my head alone. The talking helps me to stay focused and when I hear it outside of my head, I find I remember it more clearly and can work though it more easily. I do that a lot when I am walking although it is always a little strange when someone comes up on me from behind that I didn't hear coming in the middle of what seems to be a one-sided conversation. Perhaps I should just wear my Air Pods when I walk. lol.

I really can't think of any good reasons to not talk to your spouse or partner. It's a way of establishing a connection or extending one that does no harm that I can find. If it feels right for you to do it, then it has healing contained within it. If you don't feel comfortable with it, that's fine too. As with so many things in grief, what works for you, works for you and what's right for you, is right for you.

✿

Habits of Grief:

As I've written in Chapter 7, grieving isn't necessarily a bad thing, but over time, we can actually fall into habits of grieving as we do with any other repetitive task or way of thinking. By eventually breaking into those habits, by building routines and rituals that are outside of our grief or beginning to engage in life again, we can break out of our grief habits into more healing thoughts and ways of spending at least parts of our days and nights. In time, not actively grieving can become a habit and take over how we live the next part of our lives.

Questions:

- Are you taking care of yourself?

- Are you eating well and sleeping well? What might you do to help you if you are not?

- If you are using sleep aids or medications during your bereavement, are you staying aware of amounts, reactions and consequences?

- Have you considered journaling? Do you think writing about your grief and how it makes you feel would be healing, especially if it were private?

- Do you talk to your loved one?

- How does it make you feel if you do?

Chapter 9

Taking Control of Our (new) Life

Onward into
the light...

This chapter is an extension of what we discussed in the last chapter. It's another look at some of the same things in more depth as well as other things I've learned that are related to and were helpful to think about in moving forward through the reconstruction part of my journey.

I share my take on them here as much to show a commonality of experience, to let you know you are not the only one experiencing or feeling these things if you are, as to give you solutions. I really only know how it was for me, and I suspect that in this part of the journey, we each have to find our own way and find what works for us.

Taking control of our (new) life:

For many of us, I've learned and been told, the beginning of our grief journey happens in a fog. The early days, weeks and months and sometimes even years, are times when our grief is almost totally in control of our lives and we are just being pushed from moment to moment and thing to thing with little or no thought or control of our own. As time passes, we are faced with the daunting task of taking control of our lives back into our hands, of making (good) decisions and charting new directions.

Here are a few things to think about, some problems you may face, and some stories from myself and others that hopefully will help you to find your way through those times.

Picking up the pieces, taking on the tasks:

Finding continuity can be a problem anytime in our lives but within our grief-fogged brains, it sometimes seems or becomes almost impossible. The same is true for beginning to do the normal tasks that define our lives.

At some point, which is different for each of us, we will have to start putting a life together that includes all kinds of everyday things. We need to find food and bathe, we need to keep our personal space at least relatively clean, we may need to take care of children or a pet. Picking up these pieces of our lives takes concentration and energy at a time when we have so little of it to devote to these things and when even their importance is often questionable.

What was shared is now yours to find a way to do without the help and support of your spouse:

Not only do we have to do the tasks we usually did during our marriage but we now have the very difficult task of doing all the things our spouse or partner did as well. What was once a two person life still contains most of the same things, needs and responsibilities. But now it's all on us to not just do everything but in many cases to have to start from scratch and learn how to do some tasks that our spouses and partners did in the first place.

One thing I've learned is to try to find good help when you are up against things you don't know or don't know how to do. If it's possible to get recommendations from friends and neighbors or if your neighborhood maintains a list of qualified and vetted service people, it is always good to check those resources.

At least for the first time you do a new task, you may need to find someone to help or hire someone to do it and then watch and pay attention and ask questions so you can duplicate the task in the future, especially if it's a more normal, routine task like starting the lawnmower or turning on the sprinklers or cooking a turkey or doing the taxes... There is almost always a YouTube video out there to help with the material things as well.

Making decisions without your loved one:

From talking to lots of bereaved spouses and partners, this appears to be another of the hardest emotional and mental things we have to learn to do. In most marriages and partnerships, there are many shared decisions, we discuss things and we decide together what we want to do or how we want to proceed or do things. There are also the individual decisions that each of us made based on our individual roles within our marriages or partnerships. We come to depend on that sharing to find our way through all we need to decide in our shared lives.

As hard as it is to do our individual decision making during our bereavement, the need to learn to do all the decision making we used to share can be even more difficult, but it is a major step we eventually have to take going forward. Especially if the person who is no longer there was making most of the decisions about a particular part of your lives, you now have to pick up the ball and without support or help from that person, you get to figure it out and then do it by yourself.

Unfortunately, especially early in our bereavement, when we are least focused and least able to make our best decisions is when we are often required to start taking on these responsibilities and make often critical choices that effect our lives going forward. We need to learn to take on the every day decision making processes and learn to find the energy to continue doing them and try to learn to do them as well as we can even if it isn't as well as our spouse did them when they were the ones making those choices.

It can be another daunting task with no easy or convenient solutions, and here again, I believe it's ok to ask for help and allow trusted friends and family to help us make some of these decisions and also to help us to relearn how to make decisions on our own. As before, if someone else makes a decision for us, it would be good to make sure that they are decisions we approve of because in the end, we have to live with them and the consequences of them. It might be wise to allow people to help when you need it, but if possible, whenever you can, have the decisions come back to you for final approval before they are implemented so you can have the final say and control over what is done or said or promised in your name.

I can't say how you should do any of this either. It has to be something that you work out for yourself as and when you need to. I do know from what I experienced, that just knowing that it was often my grief keeping me from doing things or making me think I wasn't able to make decisions or make good choices, allowed me to begin to start denying the negative thoughts my grief was causing me to think so I could learn to make those choices for myself.

Once I began to recognize that my lack of ability to make decisions was often an illusion caused by my grieving, that it was an effect of my grief, I began to remember all the decisions I had made throughout my life and that there were many successful ones among them as well. That was the base I built upon and it allowed me to work out the rest of the details within the context of my own life and grief.

What to leave in, what to leave out:

At some point too, we all need to make decisions about what we want to retain and what we need to let go of from our old lives as we build our new ones. A tendency for many (including myself) but not everyone, is to hoard every little thing that reminds us of our loved ones and keep things pretty much exactly as they have always been.

This goes for both material items and the way our living spaces are arranged to how we navigate through our lives and the things we do, the way we do them and sometimes even the order we do them in. These can become "sacred practices" that we do to hold and retain as much as we can of our loved ones. Any deviation can seem like a betrayal and a letting go that early on is close to impossible.

But there may be and usually will be a need at some point to "clean house," to change some things to lighten the load, to emotionally and physically down size so the actual daily burden of things that need to be done is reduced so it becomes more accessible to us living alone. Remember too, as I keep writing, it's always best if it's your decision what to do and when to do it. No one else knows your emotional needs and so these are your choices to make if you can.

Ch-ch-ch-changes:

Grief has changed me! So many of my "sure of's" were lost with Andi's passing. In response, I personally found myself clinging and holding tightly to every part of our life that remained and wasn't willing or able to change anything I could keep from changing.

I wanted it all to remain static and unchanging because it kept me in contact with Andi and all the parts of our lives together. Over time, that feeling remained pretty strong in me and for each little change I did make, I felt guilty and asked Andi for permission and forgiveness for doing things as small as moving a piece of furniture or getting new towels in the bathroom.

It took me three and a half years until I was able to even consider moving Andi's clothing out of the closet. Not only was having her things in the closet intensely emotional and "sacred" to me, but also in a much more mundane sense, they were getting dusty on the back sides of the hangers and I knew she would hate that. An even less important and fairly selfish reason was that I kind of wanted more room in the closet for my stuff.

So changing things in the material world for me was a real challenge but I also know people who made all kinds of changes quite early, from not only moving to a new home or storing clothing and possessions but to giving away clothing and lots of the decorations and personal items. Some people I've talked to found their own sense of peace in quickly removing many of the items from their lives that were causing sad memories so they could move forward more easily.

It's another "no right answer" situation. What I've seen tells me that it's everyone's individual decision to make and it's only the right time when it's the right time for each of us. No one else can or should make these choices and decisions for you because it's your grief and your heart that needs to be comfortable with the choices you are making and you have to listen to your heart and let it guide you to your own personal solutions.

The larger changes, like moving and changing vehicles or redecorating the space you shared are also yours to make as well. Unfortunately for some, financial matters force decisions on us long before we are ready or wanting to make them. I have seen people go through some of these situations and it has always seemed from my perspective that they have been very sad and often confused and angry by being forced into these positions. Once it had been done, however, once they had been in their new situation for a time, they seemed to rise out of the shock and distress it caused them and find a new equilibrium that became a base line for them to then begin building on as they went forward.

I've heard it said many times that if possible, one shouldn't make major changes or decisions in the first year of bereavement. In general, that seems to be a good idea to me since we are often less than clear in our thinking and trying to relieve the pain we are in can sometimes make us do things we might not ordinarily do and not necessarily be happy we did looking back on it.

One friend told me that they sold their spouses truck and their own car and then bought a new car almost immediately. They also expressed a few years later that they wished they hadn't done that, that they would love to still have the truck to use!

Another person told me they were just feeling so lost and unsure of what to do that one day, for no apparent reason, they drove into a car dealership and on the spot, traded in their car and bought a new one. A year later they were still happy with the choice and loved the new car.

I also know two people who sold their homes within a year of their bereavement. One just felt they had to do something to move forward and the other felt that they should do it for unspecified reasons. In the end, the first one turned out to be fairly happy with the choice and the second was kind of sad and sorry they had done it and that they maybe should have waited longer before making the choice.

The point of these stories is that we are all different and it's your journey and your solutions that matter. Here, two fairly similar situations had very different reactions in the people who had been through them.

Filling the time and space you would have spent with your spouse day to day:

One of the most difficult things I remember from early in my own journey was all the empty space and time in my life as well as the often numbing level of silence that had all been previously filled by Andi. We were blessed with having spent the years of Andi's cancer journey together in a mostly retired, together-all-the-time life and spent most of our time being with each other.

On the other side of that, when my bereavement began, all of a sudden there was an awfully large void that confronted me at every turn. No matter what I did, every moment seemed to have something missing from it and it was so much more empty for Andi not being at my side.

Regardless of how much time you and your spouse or partner spent together each day, the space your loved one filled is now empty. For me, finding ways to fill those spaces was and still is one of the most difficult things I had to learn.

We just finished a new song about the silence, this is the chorus:

Numbing silence fills the air,
as clouds begin to gather,

the mists refuse to clear,
as the silence starts to shatter,
and the rain begins to thunder,
'cause I can't hear your sweet voice,
singing love songs here, anymore…

From Silence in our Lives (© Howard and Andrea Fischer, 2022).

The rebound effect:

I, as most bereaved spouses and partners do, spent a lot of time during my early grief just thinking, remembering and wishing. After a while, I began to realize that a large amount of what I was wishing for and thinking about during the lonely hours of sitting around and feeling empty, of wanting someone to talk to and be with and even my times of missing and wanting some affection, contained a lot of fantasy and illusions.

Before I realized I was doing it, I also often ended up projecting those illusions on the people I saw and met because I thought I needed someone to fill those empty spaces in my life. I thought that doing that would somehow make it better. It took even longer for me to began to understand that what I really wanted was not the illusions or the other people but it was to have Andi back filling all those spaces and needs and not someone else.

In my grief, the needs and desires for what I was missing in my physical and emotional life made me think I wanted and needed to fill those voids with another person. The reality of it was that what I really needed to do was to let those empty spaces heal on their own and let the emptiness close, scab and scar over.

Over time, it finally became clear to me that healing was what I really needed and that I couldn't just rebound into being with someone else, trying to fill up my emptiness with another person as a substitute for my wife.

As I went forward, I saw that I indeed needed to do a significant amount of healing in order to become resigned to being on my own in my material life. Only then, once I knew I could do it by myself, that I had learned enough and grown strong enough to function on my own could I even entertain the idea that I might actually have something to offer another person if I chose to. Again, I needed to heal my own self or else what did I have to give to someone else other than my grief and my needs. Grief and needs might buy me sympathy or empathy but they certainly wouldn't give me love or an equal and balanced relationship. Perhaps I didn't need another relationship at all and it was alright to live on my own. Maybe I didn't have to define myself and my new life as part of a couple again.

So some questions I had to ask myself were: Did I need to establish a new relationship because I needed to be part of a couple to define myself? Could I learn to become whole again in a new and different way while not leaving behind or denying or removing anything from my pre-grief life? Could I try something new?

This was just me, I know of people (bereaved spouses) who over time, sometimes a fairly short time, have come to find new people in their lives, have created new relationships, and have decided to build those new relationships and walk new paths together and have found healing in doing it that way. It seems to be working.

So, here too, what ever works for you is what works for you.

Insecurity and lack of self confidence:

For much of the first few years of my bereavement, I experienced a pretty strong lack of self-confidence, lots of doubts about my ability to do things. I believe it was also tied into my inertia, the not wanting to do anything, the "I can't" and the "it's too hard" and the like.

What I've come to see is that for me, it was all tied together, it was something that came at least in part from my inability in the end to save Andi and my inability to keep her from the pain she experienced and ultimately from the end of her material life.

Somehow, I had failed at the most important thing I ever wanted to do. Again at least in part, it shattered my self-confidence, if I couldn't do that most important thing, how could I succeed at anything else?

You can see how that might just take all the will out of me, keep me sitting and grieving and not believing in anything I could do to make it better or to grow in any way. It became very difficult and sometimes impossible to trust that I would ever do anything I tried with any success again, even the little things.

As time passed, and as I thought more about it and really once I was able to start defining what I was feeling and why, I was slowly able to begin to make changes in how I saw myself, how I felt about myself and eventually how I acted. I was very gradually able to begin redefining myself, to slowly begin to regrow my self-image and by spending a lot of time remembering past successes, past accomplishments, and even past triumphs, I started denying the inertia and negative places in myself that were holding me down and holding me back.

It has been a number of years of a long and often difficult journey that is still going on. I still sometimes have to struggle to remember who I am and what I can do especially when I attempt new things and walk into unknown territory and unknown situations. I have to keep reminding myself that I can and will do what I need to do, that I am capable, that I am strong, and that I can improvise through new situations based on a lifetime of successes and of overcoming past failures. I also use the I am-I can-I will mantra from one of my intent statements to help me all the time. The story of that   intent statement is in the Intent section of Chapter 5.

And while I still wish I could have changed things, made things better and ultimately saved Andi from going through what she did, I keep having to remember that it was never my fault. It was never something I could have prevented or held off; I and we did the best we could do within the situation we were faced with.

That was just how it turned out and now I need to grow, to move forward and become more, to learn and experience life again. I need to live the time I have before me and let guilt and regret and feeling responsibility for things that were out of my control slip away. I need to keep working to free my mind of illusions of things that aren't and weren't real and become myself again, free of those thoughts and feelings and move forward, become more and not let illusions of the past keep me from living and growing.

❧

Paying attention to your health, eating and sleeping:

These are three other areas most bereaved spouses or partners I've talked to struggle with early in their journey back to functionality and living on their own. It's more inertia stuff, things we don't have the energy to do and in many cases early on, can feel too sick to do. There is another discussion of some of these things in Chapter 8.

In the case of sleep, we often just can't seem to slow our thoughts down enough to relax and fall asleep or we wake and start "mind-spinning" during the night and then can't get back to sleep.

Feeding yourself well is a sort of obvious one, we need good food to stay healthy. Our grief and the accompanying feelings of depression, sickness and inertia can quickly take its toll on our physical health. Eating at all is often difficult and eating well and perhaps even cooking are sometimes impossible. But eating junk food, eating throughout the day just to get a good feeling from it, not eating or not eating enough all rob us of health and stamina to do our tasks, to stand under the onslaught of the grief waves and keeps us from moving forward in our journeys toward healing and wellness.

Our emotional health is compromised by our grief anyway. If you feel you want to use drugs, medications or alcohol to help you dull down the pain and loneliness or to help you fall asleep or remain asleep through the night, it's usually possible to do so carefully and in moderation. As I wrote about in the previous chapter, it is very important that you make sure that you remain in control of your usage. It can be way too easy to become dependent on drugs or alcohol during periods of emotional turmoil. While they may be used to advantage and to "take the edge off" it is very important that we not let them take over our lives and make us even more unable to function or move forward.

I believe it's always important to consult with a medical professional about any mind-numbing perception-drugs we may want to use and to very seriously plan and limit their usage in our lives. Prescription, and certainly recreational drugs and alcohol, too, are a potential trap that our pain and sadness can let us grab hold of and then lose control of before we know it.

Going to work and making it work, a positive look at working because we choose to do so to end the chapter:

I was mostly working online and then became fully retired through the last 10 years or so of Andi's life. I never really had to physically go to work during that time and when I became bereaved, I wasn't faced with many of the difficulties of going back to work during the earliest part of my grieving that I know can be a difficult part of that experience for many people.

But I later came to learn that working can also have positive value and help with the healing process as well.

Sometime early in my second year of grieving, my daughter called me one day and made a suggestion that profoundly changed my life and my grief journey. At that time, I was spending most of my time at home, alone, trying to engage myself with various hobbies and learning new skills and working on overcoming inertia.

My daughter is a nurse and owns and runs a CPR and Medical Assistant Training School. Her suggestion to me was that with my teaching background, she could easily train me to teach CPR and First Aid classes and wouldn't it be great if we could open a CPR School in Colorado. Uhhhh... What.... "I can barely get through the day with enough focus to do what I need to do to take care of myself and you want me to do what?"

Not a surprising response I think. But once we were done with the conversation and I had time to think it through, I realized and I'm sure she did too, that I would really gain a lot from having something structured and concrete to do, and that teaching was definitely something I already knew how to do fairly well. So, we spent a few months talking about it and conceptualizing it and that turned out to be good for me too, having to concentrate on the project was a good focusing tool.

By the start of that summer, we had actually rented a location for the school and my daughter, her husband and their office manager came out to visit and to my amazement, in 4 days, they had the entire classroom, office and files set up and ready to go and an online schedule published. And then they left and went home!

And the next week, it was all on me, I had a class scheduled, never having taught CPR before and it was "sink or swim." Well, I swam, as hard as I could for a while and managed to keep my head above water through the first few months. Pretty soon, I felt comfortable doing it and eventually got to be fairly good at it.

The important point of the story is that I think it really was one of the most important things I did to start living again, to let healing grow within me and to begin to move forward in my life. Taking on the responsibility and learning to teach the classes gave me a purpose that had been lacking although I'm not sure I realized that at the time. It also put some structure and responsibility back into my life when I really needed it.

It taught me that I could indeed function again and it gave my self confidence a much needed boost that helped me in many of the other things I've done in the years since we began the school. I'm also sure it was all part of my daughter's plan.

And, I have to smile and say that becoming business partners with my daughter and building a new adult relationship that didn't have parenting in it was an added bonus that turned out to be a wonderful gift to us both.

Questions:

- If you have begun to take on the tasks and make the decisions you used to share, what strategies have you used and how might you continue the process?

- What have you had to learn to do that you never did before? How did you figure out how to do it? Can you apply that process to other things?

- How did it make you feel when you actually did it successfully? Or not successfully?

- How are you doing at learning to make decisions on your own?

- Did you find you had (have) issues with self confidence?

- What might have caused them? Can you think of ways to overcome them if they are keeping you from moving forward?
- How do you feel about new relationships?

- Do you feel it's important to be part of a couple to be whole or complete?

- Can you think of positive or negative aspects of being on your own at this point in your life?

- What would a new life rich with friends instead of a single full-time relationship look like to you?

- What would a new relationship look like now and how would you accommodate the memories of your spouse or partner in the new relationship?

Chapter 10

Inertia

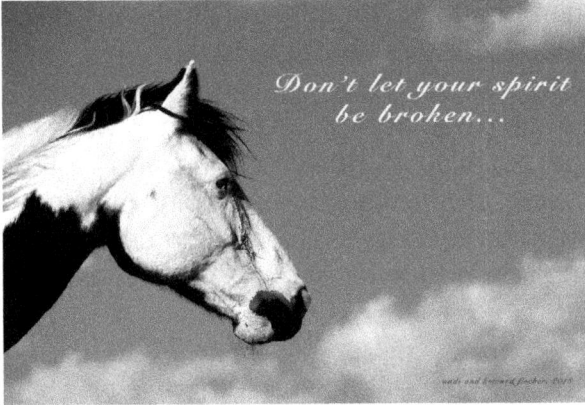

Don't let your spirit
be broken...

Inertia: An object at rest tends to remain at rest, but, an object in motion tends to remain in motion. I believe that inertia is one of the most important components of our grief and healing journeys.

Someone I spoke with recently told me they didn't like the word healing to describe what they were going through and seeking. The word functionality came up in the conversation and the person I was speaking with told me they were much more comfortable using that word, that they thought it expressed how they felt much more clearly than healing did. I find myself using that word now as well and it has made its way into this discussion as an action word, as something we can use to describe what we are trying to do in our lives.

In the context of my grief, inertia is my way of talking about a pervasive type of grief fatigue. A way of talking about the feeling of being unable to find the energy or ambition to do things, from getting up off the couch or getting dressed or even getting out of bed or of making decisions of any kind.

Especially in the early days, weeks, and months of our grief, the weight of our grief can be so heavy that we are often physically and mentally immobilized by it and find ourselves just sitting and staring or crying or remembering or not thinking at all. Any ambition to move or think seems absent and unavailable to us.

Later on, inertia can manifest in many other ways, not just as a physical lethargy but also in our emotions and in thoughts like, "I can't or I won't, or I don't want to" stopping us from doing things that we might want or need to do. So, inertia can also often manifest as a lack of ambition and a tendency to find reasons and excuses not to do things.

I believe, from my own experience, that there is an element of inertia hidden in much of our grieving. The sooner we begin to fight the inertia in all its disguises, and learn to overcome it, the sooner we will begin to find energy again to pursue all aspects of our lives. I see fighting and overcoming inertia as a major part of my own healing journey, of building my strength and my confidence to be able to live again.

With time, I believe we all need to make the effort and then learn the skills it takes to recognize and overcome that inertia and "get moving" once again as we begin the journey back to living in our new world.

It's not an easy task. It's a lot of work. It's actually easier to not work on it and let it keep us bound. I believe, however, that it's a critical task we should try to take on as soon as we can.

I've found that while inertia can ease somewhat on its own, it usually happens very slowly and gradually if at all. If we work on it, however, we can often accelerate the process and perhaps avoid letting habits of grief develop that we later have to figure out how to break.

I think maybe retired people or people who have not been working outside the home for whatever reason, may have some greater struggles with this and find it more prevalent in their lives than those who have to go to work every day but I'm not sure.

I know we all feel inertia in some way and to some extent, but it seems like when we have the time and "luxury" to stay home, especially during our early bereavement, inertia can often get the better of us. Staying in a robe all day, not eating or snacking all day, not doing anything but sitting and feeling bad, shitty actually, can become a habit, almost a way of life if we let it and don't find some reason to get moving and doing.

I'm sure that the various restrictions that happened during the COVID pandemic had an effect and also the many people who are now working from home, have been impacted as well. For months most of us were unable to really go outside our homes, and some of us continue to do that or our jobs now allow us to spend much more time at home, often alone. What little incentive we had to get up, get dressed and function as normally as we could was and is still potentially on hold.

In a way, for many of us, COVID gave us time and a situation where we could grieve at home and that might have been a positive thing in some cases. Unfortunately, inertia is also there with us to possibly gain a foothold in our lives or even to take over. If we've moved passed it, inertia can certainly reestablish itself.

Another conversation I had that illustrates a fairly extreme version of this concept was with a person who told me they had done essentially nothing for a number of years. They were so weighted down that they didn't go anywhere and didn't do much of anything. They just sat and stared in a kind of shocked silence, lost in memory, immobilized by their grief. When I met this person, it was finally at a time when they were breaking free of that immobilizing inertia and starting their journey to functionality again.

The level of inertia we experience is, as with most things, individual. Personality, circumstances, needs, work, available help and many other things seem to affect us each differently. The constant seems to be at least at some level, that our grief tends to hold us still and one of the things we need to learn is to overcome that feeling of not wanting to do anything and learn to move forward towards functionality again. Hard or easy, slow or fast, it's a major part of the healing process and the need to return to functionality which seems to be fairly common across the community of the bereaved.

In my own life, I'm not really sure why, but it became one of the most important things I worked on and tried to build during my own early grief times. It became very important for me to find some way to overcome the inertia and to gain the energy to take care of myself and the material world things and responsibilities that needed to be done regardless of my not wanting to do them.

Maybe it was because Andi was such a fighter, she never let her illness or her treatments stop her or even really slow her down much. I think how she behaved was an example of how to get through really hard times that I felt I had to live up to. Another possibility was that I was alone in the town where we were living at the time, with no family or even friends available, so essentially, it was all on me, all the time.

I ended up first spending hours and days telling myself "I needed to get up and do something." Then I spent hours and days and weeks and months focusing on "get up and do it." And gradually, things started to happen. My first big step forward was actually making myself cook a French toast breakfast one Sunday morning.

Not sure exactly how it happened but I know it began by my thinking, "you need to get off your butt and make breakfast and make French toast just because you need to do it (and not only because its good for you but because you like it)." It was a beginning!

Some of the thoughts I remember having come into my mind in those early days that were part of the inertia trying to keep me immobile were: it's too hard, it takes too long, I'm too tired, I don't want to, I'm grieving and don't have to. I'm sure there were others as well.

I still struggle to overcome those types of thoughts, to not give in to them, and then to not do something. I think I always had some of that within me, but in my grief, those thoughts amplified and became huge obstacles to movement and overcoming them became one of the most difficult but important things I had to learn.

Giving a shit!

This section came out of some things that were said and some feelings that were expressed at a support meeting I held recently. They made me remember things I hadn't felt or really thought about much in a few years. But they made me remember very clearly how important hope is in our grief and healing journeys.

It can sometimes be very hard in our grief to find the will to care about much of anything at all. To doubt that there is a good reason out there for us to even bother to try.

It is another part of inertia that, as we look at our shattered lives, at the loss of not only our love but of our futures, that we often can't see a reason to look toward the future at all. It's hard in that time to not descend into some pretty heavy hopelessness and see no reason to do much of anything.

But I believe that it's important to remember that since we are not our grief, we are grieving, it may well be our grieving that makes us feel that way. It may be another form of mental inertia. If nothing else, I believe that our loved ones would want us to carry on, to find new reasons to live and grow and maybe more importantly, if the roles were reversed, we would want those things for them!

While we sometimes can't see much reason to face and do the myriad of tasks and chores and responsibilities of living now that we are alone, part of the hope in hope and healing is that we will slowly learn to do these things despite our despair and loneliness. That we will slowly learn the skills and tasks it requires for us to go on living. And that we will also actually learn to care that we learn them.

In an image Andi sent me while I was writing this, I believe it's important to hold on through these bleak times, through the winter of our grieving, to do the work and to move forward in small steps as we can. I believe that it is important to slog through the snow no matter how tired we feel and how hopeless it looks. Until one day, out of seemingly nowhere, we see a small fire burning in the distance that we can head toward, embrace and allow its heat and light to begin to warm us and heal us. To let us find the strength within ourselves to survive, and not just to survive, but to begin to grow and live again.

Overcoming the inertia - Structure to help us return to functionality:

Rituals and routines: Establishing structure with linear patterns at first, and then when we can, becoming less structured and more non-linear in the day to day parts of our life.

A routine is something you do the same way, in the same order time after time to accomplish the same or similar outcomes. It's a way to build your life back one task at a time, one routine at a time, until you are able to function through the entire day.

I started one such routine by making that French toast breakfast every Sunday morning. Then I created a linear pattern that was very locked in for my mornings in general that consisted of getting up, taking a shower, doing a little yoga, getting dressed and having breakfast each day. I did the same things in the same order and the same way day after day, at least partly to make sure I did each part of it.

Also, the linearity and repetition made sure that I had a pattern that allowed me to include all I needed to do to get through that part of my day no matter how little concentration I was able to focus on it. From there, I slowly built my life back one task at a time, one routine at a time until I was able to function through the entire day.

Making lists and putting tasks on a calendar were a big part of how I began to create those routines. After all, there's no one here to remind me!

A ritual to me is the mental/emotional/spiritual equivalent of a routine. It's the thoughts and feelings you repeat in the same way each day or every time the same situation occurs. Every night, for example, the last thing I do before I head for bed is to stand in front of Andi's picture and talk to her, tell her about my day and then I send good energy and thoughts to all our family and friends. For me it is a peaceful way to end the day, to connect with Andi and I think it helps me to sleep more easily as well.

Early on, once I made a ritual or routine happen, I remember trying to use the same process in creating other routines, of using the same thoughts, actions and energy on each thing that came up that in my inertia I didn't want to do or was doing badly.

Once I began to move with purpose again, I saw that creating those routines was a way to get things done. I then began to establish more routines and rituals to guide me through every part of my day. I began to learn to replace my inertia and many of the patterns of my old life with new, active patterns; the rituals and routines that now helped me to find my way through the days and tasks that came before me.

After about three and a half years, (again, different for each of us) I slowly began to start relaxing some of those tightly held routines and allowing myself to become more non-linear in my actions. I began to be able to trust that I was thinking clearly enough that I could get things done no matter what order I put them in. I began to see that as long as stuff got done, I could start to do it in any order and not be so rigid and structured in my actions.

I've now begun to trust that I will intuitively (and with the help of my calendar) come to do all I need to do and don't have to so carefully and completely lay out every detail of the path first. I can be more "improvisational" about my life now that I know I have mostly mastered the ability to function most of the time and mostly don't slip back into inertia and debilitating grief. Some days I'm still a "space cadet" but I now have learned to trust that while tomorrow may be different, the habits of my routines will kick in and see me through.

Using guide words, making lists and/or putting tasks on a calendar are good ways to began to create routines and rituals. I still live off my calendar to make sure things get done and get done when they need to.

Using specific words or phrases that you can repeat over and over can help you to focus on things you want to accomplish and to build the habit patterns of routines and rituals in your mind and your actions.

Some simple examples are: I will..., I won't..., ie. I will be kind, I will make breakfast, I will clean the house. I won't sit on the couch all day and eat junk food. I won't get angry at things people say. I won't have just one more drink. I will go out to dinner alone! I will learn how to go to the grocery store without crying.

Can you think of some more complex examples?

More about the work it takes to overcome inertia:

I'm returning to this idea because it has been very important to me and overcoming it was a large part of my growth. I had to work on it almost daily from the very start.

Once I recognized inertia as something that was happening to me and as something that I needed to overcome to start moving forward in my life, whenever I would get those immobilizing thoughts like, I'm too tired, I'm too sad, I just don't want to, it's too hard, it takes too long and others of the like, I began to deny them in my mind. I kept telling myself, no, this is just inertia and no matter how I feel and what my mind tells me, yes I can do these tasks and I need to get up and do them now!

And I remember that each success led to more success and more confidence that I indeed could do things. A very positive side effect of overcoming the inertia was the rebuilding of my self confidence and my self image as a " doer," as a person who could actually get things done again. It allowed me to slowly begin to do the tasks of every day life and begin to build a basis for not only doing things but also for enjoying the doing.

As I wrote about earlier I cooked my first real meal late in the first month of my bereavement. For some reason I got up one Sunday morning thinking how nice it would be to have French toast for breakfast. Then I went through all of the "oh it's too hard, it takes too long and on and on" denials. And finally I got tired of all that, I knew I had made french toast before, it wasn't that hard and so I just got out a pan and began to make breakfast.

And it wasn't hard at all and it didn't take too long and even cleaning up wasn't nearly as difficult as my inertia told me it would be and btw, it tasted great! It was a beginning. I made it a routine. I made myself cook French toast every Sunday morning thereafter and I still do so today and I don't have to make myself do it now either, I look forward to it. And it's still good!

That was the beginning of my discovery that my mind, and sometimes my body, was telling me I couldn't do stuff and in my grief I believed it. Once I began to deny the negatives, I found out I could do pretty much everything else I wanted or needed to do once, no matter how I felt, I stopped listening to the I can't and substituted I can and I will.

Learning how to do the mundane stuff that can be so hard to do, both early on and as time passes. Finding the energy to do your normal stuff, and taking on the stuff you relied on your spouse to do:

These three statements are really one idea that is also tied to inertia.

There always has been a list of things to do in our lives but in our early grief especially, while that list continues, we have almost no energy to get up and do them. In a marriage, those things are almost always shared out between the two partners. Now, all the material tasks and jobs and repairs and that endless seeming list of things life gives us to do must be done by us, on our own. We alone have the responsibility to keep the material world needs of our lives moving forward and not allow them to stop or atrophy or deteriorate and fail because we can't find the energy to do them.

But, we can still find endless reasons to not do things too, including not really caring whether they get done or not. It's a time when those same inertia thoughts like: I can't, I don't want to, I don't know how, I won't, and it's too hard, can take us over and keep us stagnant if we let them.

But we now have a responsibility to maintain both our material world and our emotional world. We have a responsibility to keep the material world needs of our lives moving forward and not allow them to stop or atrophy or deteriorate and fail because we can't find the energy or will to do them.

We also have the responsibility to ourselves, our families, and our friends to remain as mentally and physically healthy as we can as we find a road that leads us to healing, wellness and living.

I think there's a trap here to watch for too, because if we don't begin to overcome the inertia, if we keep putting things off, the longer we wait, the more habitual the inertia becomes and the more excuses we find to keep putting things off. The longer we wait, the easier it becomes to find ever new excuses to not do things and to excuse ourselves from doing them because we are grieving, even long after our grief begins to taper off in its intensity.

I believe from my own experience, that the sooner we begin to fight the inertia and learn to overcome it, the sooner we will begin to find the energy again to pursue all aspects of our lives. I see it as a major part of my own healing journey, of building my strength and my confidence to be able to live again.

It's not an easy task and it's actually easier to not work on it and to let it keep us bound and static but I believe it's a critical task we should try to take on as soon as we can. We need to do the work and escape the hidden trap of I can't or I don't want to… turning into I won't and I don't.

Habits of grieving:

I want to add a short note here at the end of the chapter about something I briefly mentioned at the end of Chapter 8 that can happen if we are not careful or aware and that is something that it is all too possible to find ourselves doing and being. Using as an example watching movies for hours each day because we can't find the energy to do anything more active, I have talked to people who have fallen into a pattern where that's what they do almost every day.

In our grief and inertia, patterns like that can easily repeat themselves day after day. As with anything repetitive, they can become habits of action and thought. They can then take on a life of their own and keep us locked into those patterns. Changing those patterns becomes ever more difficult with time.

I call these places "habits of grief." I believe it is important to periodically examine our actions if we can. If they appear habitual and repetitive and fairly non-productive and are beyond what are intentional, healthy routines, if they go on and on, it would be good to try and make the effort to break out of them and pull the wheels of our lives out of those well-worn ruts and into new pathways of healing and growing and moving forward. There is more about habits of grief in Chapter 14.

Some questions:

- Do you feel inertia in your life?

- If you do, how does it happen, what does it feel like and sound like in your thoughts?

- Are you struggling to find not just the energy but the ambition to do things?

- What specific thoughts do you have that keep you from doing things?

- What do you and can you do when you feel and think these things?

- What might you do going forward to keep inertia from stopping your healing and growth?

- Do you think you are locked in any habitual grief patterns or thoughts? What do you think you can do to change them if you choose to?

- Have you begun any new activities and things to occupy yourself?

- What would it take to break out of your inertia and begin to do new things?

- What have you always wanted to do that you may not have had time to do in the past?

- Could you find a way to do that now?

- Would establishing routines help to overcome the inertia?

- Would or does making lists and writing on calendars help?

- Would you be willing to try to establish a routine to see how it works?

- Can you think of any words or phrases that might help you to build routines?

- Can rituals help keep a connection with your loved one and perhaps bring some continuity into your life?

- Do you think you need to be "proactive" in approaching the building of your "new" life?

- How might you do that?

Chapter 11

Dealing with External Expectations

KINDNESS IS A GIFT
THAT MOVES GRACEFULLY IN ALL
DIRECTIONS...

ROCKY MT. NATIONAL PARK, CO.
SILVERDREAMSTUDIO
LOVELAND, CO.
SEPTEMBER, 2013

As in the previous chapter, some of these topics are similar to things I've written about before. I am trying to look at them here from another perspective and in a bit more detail. Some of it I experienced myself and some I've asked for other people's experiences to guide me.

Dealing with external expectations:

If you are not totally isolated during your grieving, you will be interacting with people in all parts of your life. It sometimes seems as though everyone has expectations of how you should be, what you should do and when you should do it. Much of it is well intentioned I believe, but unfortunately, there may also be people who have their own agendas and want you to do or be something for their purposes.

One way or another, it seems to me that in the end, you are the one who has to live with all the decisions made and all the consequences of those decisions. It is you to whom all the changes are happening and it is your expectations and needs that should be the most important ones.

Many people, with the best of intentions, often believing they are helping you, tend to impose their expectations on you by the way they act, how they treat you and talk to you and sometimes even by telling you what to do or when to do it. Some may want you to grieve quickly and "get over it" and become your old self as soon as possible in a way that is the least difficult for them to understand or deal with.

No matter what the reasons, all these expectations are things we have to deal with and find ways to cope with and work with or around. Some are easy and match our own inclinations while others are much more difficult and can seem to be and actually are hurtful and not in our best interests.

I have no easy answers about how to recognize which of these you are dealing with. As with so many things in grief, it's usually best to go with your feelings, to do it the way that feels best to you, and in what you see as your own best interests. Whenever possible, it's probably good to try to do things only when you are ready and comfortable doing them if you can manage it, no matter what anyone suggests or tries to require you to do.

There are also situations you may encounter at work, or financially, or with family, when you don't have as much choice as you want or need. Sometimes you just have to go with the needs of the moment. When you do have a choice, however, it seems from everyone I've talked to, that it is always best to make your own choices and decisions if you can and if you're not ready to decide, then hold off as long as you can until you know what to do.

Here's a quote from Tom, one of the facilitators in my Greeley support group:

"The best advice here is to defer as much as possible for at least the first few months after the death of a loved one. For those things that just can't wait, consult with, and rely on, close, trusted family members before making any major life or financial decision."

Get back to work and get over it! NOT!

The "get over it" idea seems to be something I run into pretty often in my conversations with other bereaved spouses or partners. Whether it's about going back to work or just about not talking or crying about it anymore, there seems to be a lot of often unconscious pressure from people who have not been bereaved to have us put our grief behind us. They want us to not be hurting or sad and to get back to normal, to be the way we always had been and not bring our grief out in public.

They may very well not understand what is happening to us and how little control we sometimes have and that we would probably like it to stop even more than they would. They don't know that it's often not in our control and it just happens when it happens.

They very likely don't understand that our talking about our grief and our loved ones is part of what we need to do to heal and that telling our stories, sometimes over and over is one way we have of relieving some of the intolerable stress and aching sadness that grief brings into our lives.

Looked at from another perspective, there is a tendency for western medicine and western thinking in general to consider death, or someone dying as a failure. Western medicine is structured to prevent dying at all costs and to make every attempt to stop death from happening. A corollary to that way of thinking is a general feeling that there is also something inherently pathological about grief; after all, it makes us hurt and sad and often restricts our ability to function.

I understand that there may be aspects of long-term, extreme grief that can be so debilitating that they do need medical attention. Those places are very different and more extreme than what most people experience and that level of grief is not what I'm referring to here.

As an extension of the feeling that grief is pathological if it goes on too long, when someone grieves for longer than people feel they should, when they don't "get over it" and return to normal behaviors quickly, is, that in general, many people seem to act as though they feel that we are somehow "ill" and not dealing with our bereavement in a "strong" and healthy way.

So, expressing our grief, in a way helps to educate the non-bereaved, it helps them see what we are going through. The more of us who show our grief, the more people see it and the more people come to understand that it is a long journey to hope and healing. They may still be uncomfortable and uneasy with our expressions of grief but as with grief itself, over time, the discomfort can fade and understanding grow in its place.

It seems to me that it's mostly the bereaved themselves and I suppose people who study grief, who actually have a realistic idea of what we are going through.

In some way, in our interactions with those who don't know, it would be good if we could educate the non-bereaved to the idea that grief is a normal part of our love and of our lives and also of what is now no longer a part of our lives. I think it is important to let people know, to explain when we can, that our grief continues way past what might be expected or wanted. That we most of all would like to have our grief turn to healing and wellness and maybe even come to an end.

Much of the disconnect seems to me to be associated with the general feeling that one shouldn't dwell on problems, that one should be strong and move forward as soon as possible and that we should certainly keep these things to ourselves. It appears to be related to ideas that we should be stoic and keep our emotions private and always appear strong and in control especially when we are in public, if not all the time.

This seems especially to apply to men and sometimes women too, of a certain generation. I remember talking to one older man about crying being a good release of emotions and his response was, "I don't know how to cry. I've never done it, it was never allowed in my life growing up or since." I've recently learned that it can also be a cultural imperative to not show grief and other emotions in public.

I had another person tell me that everyone in their family and their close friends as well would stop them every time they expressed any grief behavior. They would immediately do something like shake their finger and say "uh-uh none of that. You have to be strong and get over it...." When I met that person, it was close to two years into their bereavement and they were extremely suppressed and I thought desperately in need of some affirmation about what had happened in their life. That it was ok to grieve and then to be allowed to do so.

That person had just joined a support group when I met them and has since become quite active in the group and in some of the social activities associated with it. As far as I can tell, that person is much more open about their grief now and seems to have found a much more productive and positive healing journey.

Yet another story that I've actually heard a number of times and one that seems to be fairly common, came from someone who said that they did not want to let their family and especially their children see them grieve. They felt and had been taught that a parent always needs to appear strong and that somehow the children should never know that mom or dad is hurting and needs to feel it and show it, especially with family.

Unfortunately, there may be unforeseen consequences, especially to our children and grandchildren seeing us grieve, that we may want to consider. If you haven't read that story yet, I refer you to something I heard and learned from my granddaughter that is in Chapter 5.

Unfortunately, attitudes about not showing our grief in public, while fairly common, put pressure in two directions. First, they get in the way of an individual expressing their grief and letting off some of the pressure. Second, they effect how the non-bereaved deal with bereaved people. Those attitudes tend to make people not understand that our expressions of grief are not usually something we can control or that if we find ways to control them and suppress them, we may be doing ourselves more harm than good and actually may prolong the process of healing.

At the same time, if we don't show our emotions and/or our grief, if we don't let people see us grieving, then they get the impression that we're fine, that we're ok. By not showing our grief, we give a distorted picture of what grief is and how it effects us.

And, in turn, for us, not expressing our grief makes it hard to get or ask for help now or later down the road if we need it, because everyone thinks we're fine and that we're "over it" and they don't understand why suddenly, seemingly out of the blue, we "relapse" and show our grief and that maybe we are really not (and really never have been) ok.

I think it is very important that we empower ourselves to grieve and show our grief for as long and in what ever healthy ways we need to, despite what anyone else feels is right or good for us (or them) or how uncomfortable they may be with our mourning! However, it's another "no always right answer" situation, and we may also want and need to weigh the possible consequences to others, especially children, of when, where, and how we choose to express our grief.

❀

Why are you telling me that:

Many people really don't know what to do or say to a bereaved person. They probably want us not to be hurting or sad and want to help somehow and to make us feel better. Often, because they don't really know what to say or do, there can be a large disconnect between what they feel and mean to express and the way they express it. In our grief, this can be compounded by the way we take what they express.

No matter how we feel, we still have to be out in the world at some point and we will all experience interactions with other people, many of whom have little or no idea of what we are going through. Many (most) people have very little information about what things are appropriate and what things are not.

Another quote from Tom:

"Good people can say incredibly cruel things. The best way I found to handle this is to know that you are hearing what they say through a shroud of grief and what you heard is not necessarily what they said (or intended to say). This mindset allowed me to quickly forget or forgive an insensitive comment."

Since they often don't have much information, we may need to help them (at least the people we know) to find ways to express their caring and concern that are a better fit with what we need to hear in our grieving. And on our side, we are often so raw and so emotional that almost anything can start us crying. It can also make us angry when something someone said sounds insensitive or even cruel whether it was or not, whether it was meant that way or not.

There is also an aspect of this that may be about the person saying insensitive things because at some level they are uncomfortable with our emotional expressions. Their not wanting us to show our feelings in public saves them the discomfort of dealing with it. Because they often lack a comfortable way to react, that just adds to their discomfort. Unfortunately, they may just want us to not put them in a position where they have to deal with that uncomfortable situation.

The work environment can be particularly difficult because we indeed have a job to do when we are there and it often requires our full concentration to do it well. When we are distracted by our grief, when we cannot focus and pay as much attention as we should to our work, it will probably make those tasks suffer and we will do them less well and possibly make errors of judgement.

I talked to someone who drove a long-haul truck for a living. He was required to get behind the wheel and drive a coast-to-coast run within the first week of being bereaved. He said it was terrifying to realize that for many miles of the trip, for minutes or even hours while driving, he became lost in his grief and couldn't remember were he had been or what he had done while driving that huge rig. And he had no choice. The job and the people he worked for had no understanding of his needs or his level of distraction and they never thought to relieve him until he could resume working with his full concentration on what he was doing.

In another conversation, a person I talked to told me they were given a simple alternative by their employer; stop grieving and get back to normal or you're fired! Seems pretty brutal and cruel to me but the person at least knew enough to know they wouldn't be able to, nor want to stop grieving, so they left the job...

Time to Grieve:

I believe that it would be to all of our benefits if we could be given time away from work to grieve if we wanted or needed to. The very early and most debilitating times of our grief and mourning could then be spent at home, letting ourselves fully grieve for a while before we have to go back to anything requiring our full attention.

In some older societies, grief and mourning were often a year long period of time given to the bereaved. They were not asked to do anything but mourn for that time and were supported by the community with food and help until the time of mourning was past and they then returned to their place in the community. This is not very practical or likely in today's world but it illustrates what earlier societies understood about the grieving process that we seem to have forgotten.

I think it's important to add here, from another perspective, that I've talked to people who said that going to work actually was the best thing for them. It forced them into putting their grief on hold for that part of each day and made them focus and "keep it together." If they had been home or alone, they would not have had to be strong or suppress their outward expressions and would have spent more time actively grieving and they were grateful for the time at work when they had to, for the most part, put their grief aside for a while.

After having a discussion about going back to work at a support group meeting and listening to what people there had to say about going to work, I need to add that at least for the group at that meeting, there was a strong feeling that going to work was, for them, a mostly positive thing. One person also talked about their mother telling them that she "needed" to go back to work after her husband passed, that staying home alone in the house and not having people to be with and talk to was going to be much worse than working.

Others shared that being at work was a time to not be alone with their grief and especially when they had a sympathetic boss or coworkers, that they found the time at work to be a good distraction from their grief. Those same people said that knowing they were going to be home alone on the weekend after being with people at work all week was not something they were looking forward to at all. A number of them also said that they were going to miss the presence of people and the interactions that made the days less lonely and that going home to the silence and emptiness of the house was something they were dreading.

Another person I talked to said that since they were not sleeping much and were feeling terrible sitting around the house every day, that they might as well be at work. They talked about someone at work who was also bereaved sitting around crying all day but due to the nature of their job, they had to put a smile on their face, and deal with the public and didn't have the "luxury" of not appearing cheerful because the job required it.

Yet another way to think about it is that there is structure in working. There is a need or requirement in working at most jobs that you have to do things in a fairly linear way. The various tasks of the job often must be completed in a way that creates a pattern to the day that is often repeated each day we are at work.

This patterning is an external example of what I've written about as creating rituals and routines in Chapter 10. In some ways it's a good model for restructuring our lives outside of work as well. If we use the creation of routines, the making of lists, the keeping of a calendar of our appointments at work and doing tasks in the same way time after time that may be part of our ability to do our jobs, perhaps we can use these as a model for doing stuff at home.

Perhaps these things can help us find ways to do the tasks at home that living requires us to do. If we plan our days at home the way we would at work, maybe we can allow that structure to help us to find our way back to functionality in our everyday lives.

One more time, there is no right answer here. In this one, it is often a need and not a choice that brings us out into the world and especially into the workplace. Grief isn't perceived or treated like pregnancy, we don't get bereavement leave most times as we might get maternity leave.

If you still need to be working and it's difficult, it is just something you may have to learn to find your way through. You may need to learn to adjust to it and do your best at doing enough to keep your job regardless of how it makes you feel. Perhaps you can also find a way to educate your bosses and co-workers to your needs. This may be an important time to become part of a support group or seek professional counseling to help you find your way through a difficult situation.

Yet another suggestion from Tom:

"When you have to work, and your employer can't or won't honor the time you need to grieve,   (it might be good if you) use whatever resources you have available. This could include vacation, sick leave, and coworkers taking on some of your work to give yourself as much time as possible."

❀

More about people we encounter probably having little or no idea of what we are going through and really not knowing what to do or say:

Though this is a difficult story for me to tell, it illustrates how little I knew or understood about grief and about how to express my feelings about someone's bereavement until I experienced bereavement myself.

A number of years ago, I got a message from a friend that the wife of another mutual friend had been killed in a car accident while she was out jogging. I hadn't been in contact with that person in a few years, I had moved to a new job and a new town and we hadn't kept in touch but I called him to express my condolences. I talked to him for awhile and while I don't remember much of the conversation, I do remember feeling like he didn't understand what I was trying to say and he wasn't much interested in what I had to offer and I was pretty turned off by the whole conversation.

Looking back though, in light of my own bereavement, I believe I acted and spoke as a total jerk. I totally didn't understand what he might have been feeling, and certainly didn't understand grief. I was totally self-absorbed in my side of the conversation and probably not only didn't give him any real compassion or caring, but more likely, I just ticked him off, caused him more pain and left him thinking what a fool I was.

I've regretted that for years and every now and then think about sending him a message with an apology and regret for my insensitive comments and feelings. I think I am still too embarrassed by how I acted to do it but it may yet happen if I can find the right way to express my current feelings and what I've learned from my own bereavement.

Someone recently reminded me that making amends may sometimes have enough of a selfish motive to it that it may cause yet more hurt instead of the healing we may want. It may also open wounds that have been closed for a long time. Hmmm. Another hard-to-find a right answer situation... But, perhaps working towards self-forgiveness is at least something I can do as part of my healing journey and is also probably desirable to do that long before I seek to make amends outside myself.

What I take from this yet again, is that so many people, especially those who, like myself at that time, had not been through a bereavement, just plain don't know what to do or say. Our society is not very forthcoming about grief and if it hasn't happened to you, it can be hard to gain much sensitivity to other people's needs during their grieving.

Most people, I believe, would do and say caring and kind things but too many of us just don't know what is appropriate and what is not under those circumstances. Many people fall back on cliches, like "they are in a better place," that may or may not make the bereaved feel better at all.

Another place I learned something important about expressing our feelings to bereaved people was in a mental health first aid class I attended. The class wasn't about grief but one of the things that was stressed in the class was for people to use appropriate and sensitive words and phrases when speaking about mental health. There are many ways and words used in talking about these issues that have become stigmatized and are now considered quite cruel and insensitive to use.

When I started thinking about it, I realized that the mental health community has a very large support system out there. That system helps to inform and educate the public about how we now think about mental health issues and about ways to change our language to use more sensitive and appropriate wordage.

In many ways the bereavement community doesn't have such an advocate system in place. The general public is not being well-educated in how we need to be addressed and what things are hurtful and painful for us. They aren't being educated about better ways to communicate with the bereaved in their expressions of condolence and also in ways to allow the bereaved to grieve publicly as we make our way back into our daily lives.

As we go back to work and do simple things like going to the store, that are often laced with emotional triggers that can instantly transport us into uncontrollable expressions of grief, these things are still very difficult for others to understand and react to in a positive way.

Words or phrases we would or would not want to hear:

Because I know there are many things that people say that make us less than pleased and other things we would like to hear that we often don't, I asked at a couple of support group meetings what things would people want or not want to hear other people say. These are some of the responses from that group and from other conversations I've had along the way.

It's probably important to keep in mind here, that the context of the comments we hear can affect their meaning as can the way in which they are said. So too, the effects of our grief can sometimes alter the meaning and tone of what others have said in our minds.

Things we don't necessarily want to hear:

- How was your day? How are you doing? How are you feeling? (should we respond honestly?)
- They are in a better place.
- This too will pass.
- Aren't you glad it's over?
- You will meet someone else.
- You just need to find/enter another relationship, get another person to fill the space and it will all be ok.
- Someone putting your name in a dating app on the internet.
- Having people trying to or actually taking over your life, offering or even demanding to manage your finances or how and where you live.
- People suggesting that it's time to clean out the old stuff from your life/home and offering unwanted help for you to move forward. "Let me know when I can come over next weekend and we can do that."
- You should be or I thought you were over it by now.
- Are you still going to those support group meetings?
- People turning the conversation to how they feel and making it about them.

Things that would be helpful to hear or experience:

- If someone said nothing and then just let me ramble and cry.
- If someone would just hug me and hold my hand and let me talk.
- What would your spouse have wanted for you?
- To have people talk about and remember your spouse with you.

- Someone to take the time to ask you questions about your relationship and your spouse and maybe some special times you want to recall.

- Having understanding people in the workplace who give you the time and space you need to grieve in.

- Your boss tells you to feel free to close your door and cry or what ever else you need to do.

- Encourage the non-bereaved to let it be all about you!

Are there other things or comments you might add to either list?

When people stop listening:

Since for most of us, our grieving goes on much longer than the non-bereaved think it will or should, at some point, some of our friends, co-workers and even family members seem to get tired of hearing our stories and would rather that we stopped talking about it. They may continue to listen out of niceness or they may not. They may use a variety of ways to get us to stop publicly expressing our grief, from the kind and gentle to the abrupt and not so gentle. They may also just stop listening or wanting to listen.

But our need to tell our stories, repeatedly if necessary, is an important part of our healing process. Expressing our feelings, talking about our loved ones, getting the intense emotions outside of us by sharing them are all very important things we need to do to allow ourselves to heal and grow and move forward.

Sharing our grief and our stories helps us in so many ways and I think we know it instinctively, we want to talk about our loved ones and our feelings. At some level we know that by sharing them we can dilute the pain and the sadness and work through it on our road to hope and healing.

But again, as with so much of this discussion, many people don't know that. Many people grow tired and uncomfortable hearing about our grief for very long. At some point, they may begin to shut us off, stop listening or wanting to listen.

As I've written before, I have to assume that at some level, our pain may be uncomfortable to them, especially when it lasts a long time. But I also have to think that they want us to be over it because they care about us and don't want us to be hurting any more.

What people often tell me about these types of interactions is that what they and others experience is a mutual turning away. Friends and even family become less willing to visit or talk on the phone, they become less willing to spend time talking to us or listening to us tell our stories.

There is a gradual or abrupt reduction or end to relationships that seems to not be uncommon. The bereaved are left more isolated than ever, often not understanding and hurt by what happened or why people have seemingly changed and/or abandoned them. It seems that not only the non-bereaved but the bereaved as well, need to be aware that these changes in relationships may occur all too frequently.

And so there can also be a similar reaction on the part of the bereaved when they can tell that someone is tired of listening to their stories. They can often tell that the other person doesn't care anymore and so the bereaved themselves turn away and let the relationship thin or end.

This is a time and a situation during our bereavement that can be greatly aided by finding or even starting some type of support group or social group of bereaved people who understand the situation. To find or start a group of and for people who all need most of the same things and who are willing to share their stories and journeys to help each other in their healing and growth. I've written about support groups and social groups and about how a local group of bereaved spouses came together for mutual support and benefit in Chapter 4.

What do we do when people don't know what to do or say or say stuff that makes us "crazy?"

I had the amazing experience a few years ago of being asked by two young friends if I would be willing to officiate at their wedding ceremony. I was totally shocked and honored that they held me in such high regard. Of course I agreed and went about the process of becoming ordained as a minister in the Universal Life Church to become licensed to perform the ceremony legally in our state.

After the ceremony, I joined about a hundred guests for a very lovely party to celebrate the occasion. As part of my comments at the beginning of the ceremony, I was talking about how I had met the couple and that it had happened less than a month after I became bereaved. The sensitivity they showed me at that time was greatly appreciated and became the start of our continuing friendship.

But in telling the story of how we met, I also told everyone at the wedding that I was bereaved (it was about two years at that time) and so, a large number of people came up to me at some point during the evening and expressed their sorrow for my loss. Everyone was kind and yet everyone expressed themselves differently.

It might have been very difficult to keep myself from crying and losing it each time someone else came up to me since I was still pretty raw emotionally most of the time. What I decided to do was to kind of "flip the script." Instead of having a grief reaction each time someone talked to me, I decided that instead, I would try to make each person as comfortable as I could. I would try to help them to say the right thing back to me and not make them unsure of themselves by having to face my grief.

I tried to say something kind that acknowledged what each person was expressing and also, I reacted to it in a positive way no matter how it was expressed. I worked very hard to keep myself from crying as I talked to them. I was the minister after all...

And it seemed to have worked. I wasn't crying and I was able to make them feel good for having made me feel good. Seems to have been a good plan!

Recently, a friend told me that they found a way to help themselves deal with other peoples comments that seemed insensitive by trying to understand that those people were possibly having a bad day themselves. Maybe even a worse day than they were. So it was important for them to let it go and not make any judgments about the comments, to just let the person making the comment be themselves and not take it personally if it didn't seem to send the right message.

Finding ways to explain how we feel and why it's so hard to do seemingly simple things:

So far in this chapter, I've written mostly about other people's reactions to our grieving. Well, is there a way that we can change the culture for them? How can we react to others in our heavy grief when we are most sensitive to what people do or say that may be better able to help them understand what we are experiencing?

Later, when we are healing and can look more objectively at how people interact with us and respond to our grief, can we help them to know what we need to hear?

What can we learn to do and how can we explain to others what it feels like, why we cry, why we need to talk about it sometimes much longer than people think we need to? How can we learn to tell them what they can do to help us through our bereavement even when it takes us a long time?

I remember once asking another bereaved person how their day was and they angrily answered, "you never ask that of a bereaved person." I was kind of surprised, I almost always ask that when I greet someone, its just a nice, easy way to say hello and start a conversation. However, I'm sure that person is not the only one who feels that way about those types of comments since it's on the list I shared of things people don't want to hear.

But, I personally don't feel offended when someone asks it of me, I just reply with as honest an answer as I can, often it's something like "pretty shitty thank you". Hopefully, they laugh and if they really want to know more, I can tell them or we can go on to other things. I think for myself that honesty is way better than saying the expected "fine thanks and you?" I also have to wonder if the reaction I got from the bereaved person came from their not feeling like they could be honest and tell me what they were really feeling.

In the end, it seems to me that it does little good to be angry at what people say, although anger is always a possible reaction, especially early in our grief. It seems to me that there are things to be learned on both sides of the conversation.

I wonder if it's possible for us to think it out in advance. For awhile it may not be how we normally communicate, but maybe we need to think of a more honest "standard answer" for those common greetings. Maybe we need to understand that people don't think about or know how those comments may make us feel and so we need to give them some slack and then when we can, tell them what or why that wasn't a good thing to say and give them an alternative if they want one.

Our sensitivity and our deep hurt, however, often make rational responses and thoughtful planning of our responses difficult or even impossible. If we find ourselves constantly annoyed or angered by things people say, it's possible that we may need to take a moment (or longer) and ask ourselves why we feel that way. Maybe we need to try to learn what we can do to make the situation better, to help ourselves and those who don't really know how we feel and not just react in anger or with other negative emotions. My counselor Lori used to ask me "what did that say about you" when I expressed anger over something someone said. "What did you learn from that?"

Explaining why we can't stop crying:

I want to also include the idea that especially early in our bereavement, crying and hurting and sadness are not something we can control well most of the time. I know for myself that for many reasons, in many situations, the waves of grief just came over me.

A word, a familiar place, seeing a picture or some powerful memory object or place; any of these would trigger that feeling. Then the grief would well up inside me, it would crash over me and I would be in tears and my rational self was banished to the background. All I could do then was to let the wave break, let it do its worst and then when it receded, I would take a deep breath, wipe my eyes and nose and go on. It was good through those times to always carry tissues or a handkerchief.

Those moments for me were not only uncontrolled and uncontrollable, as I've written before, they were totally not rational, they were entirely emotional and visceral and there was nothing I could think or plan that would stop them from happening. They are also a normal and important part of the grieving process. I believe they need to be allowed to happen to let some of the pain out, to take some of the stress off and allow us some relief while we move forward towards healing and wellness.

People don't know that!

If you haven't been bereaved, there are very few things like this you would have encountered and very few ways of understanding what it is like for the person experiencing it and how out of control those moments truly are.

It's another one of the things that it would help to figure out how to explain to people, especially if it happens to us when we are with other people. It's even more difficult when people don't know our situation and why this is happening.

We are trapped a bit here too, because until the wave passes and let's us go, we usually can't stop it and certainly can't take the time to explain. I found that when it happened to me, all I could do was surrender to it, go through it to the end, and when it was done, try to explain what had just happened. After finding my way through an explanation a time or two, I was able to recognize what worked and I began to use the same explanation, that I was having an uncontrollable grief moment, each time it happened. That seemed to help others understand what I was experiencing and what they had just witnessed.

Taking a "grief moment:"

Those of us who are older often talk about "having a senior moment" when we forget something or forget to do something. It's a nice and easy way to transition through the uncomfortable moment of forgetfulness and most times brings instant understanding from the people we are dealing with at the time. It often brings a laugh as well.

It seems to me that when our grief comes over us in a public situation, at an inconvenient time and place, that we should be able to "take a grief moment." We should be able to turn away or walk away and get the release we need, to cry or be unfocused or what ever other mourning behavior we find ourselves expressing.

Once the wave has passed, we can return to our activity and just be able to say, as I did a number of times in my own journey, "I was having a grief moment" and move on with little or no discomfort and perhaps more understanding on both sides. Once we have gotten through to that point and we have some self control back, if we need to, we can explain more about the uncontrollable nature of what we are going through.

Places that trigger our grief:

It seems like anyplace we go that puts us in a situation we may have shared with our loved ones is a potential grief trigger. One of the most common places people tell me about is the grocery store. Shopping together, picking a special, favorite item, memories associated with the entire experience all seem to bring on the waves.

Many people have told me about breaking down and crying in the store and some have even talked about just leaving the cart in the isle and bolting for the door to get out of there and not breaking down around a bunch of strangers. They just needed to get away from the triggering situation so they could calm down. Sometimes they go back and continue shopping and sometimes they just sit in the car, reach the end of the wave and then go home. Some have just chosen to avoiding the entire issue by doing online shopping and home delivery of their groceries.

While the grocery store is a common triggering location and it serves as an example of what happens, almost anyplace or any activity that was shared and was a source of connection or enjoyment is a possible trigger and can set us into having that grief moment.

Since we all grieve in our own ways and times, I think we also need to find our own coping mechanisms in these situations. We do need to go out into the world and especially, as with the grocery store, we do need to shop for food. These moments of heavy grief do seem to come on us less often and with less intensity as time goes on. In the very raw, early days of our grieving though, they are definitely more likely and more common.

As we go forward, we become better able to face going to these common places and doing the common activities and not have them trigger our grieving so strongly as to be debilitating. We all seem to gradually become able to resume those parts of our lives. Time is our friend here and through time, we become less raw and it becomes more possible to have these experiences without them generating such intense feelings and reactions.

❀

Why we need to keep talking about it and sharing our stories:

Everyone at some level needs to tell their stories, to validate their lives and share who and what they are and believe with other people. That seems to be part of living. For the bereaved, especially the newly bereaved, telling our stories is a way of retaining our connections with our loved ones. It gives us a chance to sooth our aching hearts by remembering and even by working through unresolved feelings and thoughts.

By telling others of our spouses or partners, we keep their memories fresh, we honor them with the stories we tell and there is a dilution of the pain by the sharing of it. Especially when we are with a group of fellow bereaved spouses or partners, when we cry together or hug each other in our common understanding of the pain we are feeling, when we share experiences from our journeys, we help each other also to validate our feelings and know we are not alone though we feel so isolated in our bereavement.

But by just telling our stories once or twice, or for a short time at the beginning of our bereavement, we can never release all the emotion or pain. A lifetime of love and connection can't be described or shared in just a short time. So we talk about it and talk about it, each time perhaps opening a new memory, sharing a new story.

As with everything in grief, over time, through repetition, we slowly and gradually begin to smooth the raw edges and sooth the worst of the pain. As that happens, our needs to talk, to re-live and to share these stories also gradually recedes and we need to do it less often. But the time it takes to get to a place of relief is different for each of us and much longer than most people expect it to be if they have not been bereaved themselves. So we continue to grieve, we continue to talk about it and we continue to look for hope and healing.

I come back here at the end of this chapter to the idea of joining together with a group of fellow travelers who all understand these things. The bereaved understand that we need to talk and that we need to share our stories and honor our loved ones.

If we can find ways to come together and share the pain and sorrow and support each other, whenever we can do so, we will find willing listeners and others who "get it" who know why we cry and tell our stories. And we can help each other to find hope and healing and slowly begin to find new meaning and purpose in and for our lives. To go forward, perhaps as new friends, together seeing a future and moving towards it, what ever it looks like and what ever it contains.

Some questions:

- What have you heard that was insensitive, inappropriate, just plain cruel and/or really made you angry?   How did you react? How might you learn to find a healthy way to deal with those types of comments?

- What do you think would be a good way for you to help people understand how you need to grieve and maybe help change how they react or respond?

- What might you say to someone that might help them be more sensitive to your needs?

- What might you think of in advance to say to someone who says something you think is inappropriate that might help the situation and not have it be fueled by anger?

- What are the best things someone said or did? How did they make you feel? How did you react?

- What would you like people to say and do to/for you when they encounter your bereavement for the first time?

- Has how you might react to another bereaved person changed since you experienced your own bereavement? What might you say or do now that is different?

Acceptance and Wellness

Chapter 12

Support: Who's There for You?

FRIENDS..

LAUGHING GULLS, ST. GEORGE ISLAND, FL.

SILVERDREAMSTUDIO
LOVELAND, CO.
AUGUST, 2013

Support, who's there for you:

This appears to be quite different for each of us and also different with each of the people we know. Some of the things I've talked to people about are how, in a lot of instances, people who knew us as part of a couple and we ourselves for the same reasons, become uncomfortable when we aren't with our spouses when we get together.

Often, all of us are uncomfortable with that dynamic, especially when we don't know how to react or what to say, when we don't know what to do when that "third wheel feeling" that something is missing enters into the interaction. Often too, if one partner was very much the more social one in a marriage, if that person is no longer there, it can be very difficult to pick up the social connections and responsibilities without them. Until we learn how to connect with people by ourselves, many of our old and certainly no new social interactions work well or in many cases are even possible for us to maintain or form.

Old friends:

As part of the grieving process and often as a result of our bereavements, many people find that old friends drop away, at least in part because they don't know how to act or aren't comfortable with us as single persons when they knew us as part of a couple. Very often, they don't know what to say or if it's ok to remember and talk about our loved ones. Their discomfort and their really wanting us to go back to being the person they remember and knew sometimes makes them withdraw their company and support in our lives, either slowly or quickly depending on who they are, what the relationship was and what they feel.

There are also those old friends who stick by us and learn to listen to our stories and who are willing, no matter when or for how long it goes on, to share our journey and hug us when we need it and let us cry if that happens. They have somehow thankfully overcome any discomfort they may have had and remain the friends they have always been.

We may also find ourselves withdrawing from old friendships as we lose commonality with those people we knew as couples and those who have not experienced what we have and who say or do things that end up being hurtful to us even when they might only have been trying to help.

Again, our society doesn't often give people much help in dealing with grief and because it is often hidden or so little talked about, most people really don't know what to say or do or how to act around a bereaved person. It may be especially obvious when your bereavement continues beyond a relatively short time and when people want you to stop talking about it. Then, the "get over it" thoughts begin to surface in other peoples minds and they may start to withdraw. There is more on this in the previous chapter.

Under these circumstances and others we might encounter, many of us find that we can become isolated and estranged from friends and support systems in our daily lives and sometimes even from family members who don't know what to do or say as time goes by and we are still grieving.

❀

Making New Friends:

One of the first tasks I set for myself as I began to overcome the worst of my inertia and move forward in my bereavement, was the making of friends. I realized fairly early that since I had no family and actually no friends at all living nearby, that I was going to have to develop a support system and a group of friends I could visit with and call on for help if I needed it, and who could also call on me in the same way.

If you are surrounded by good, supportive friends and family, this section may only peripherally apply to you or your journey, but in case it does resonate, I want to share what I did and what I learned along the way.

Since I used to be a fairly shy person when I found myself in a purely social situation, I was kind of worried at first that I would indeed become isolated and not have anyone to talk to or call on for help in an emergency. The building of friendships and just the act of meeting new people was a major undertaking for me, especially on my own. It was filled with fears and insecurities that I needed to face and overcome in order to learn to be friendly and social with people I didn't know.

How do you even do that? How and where do you meet people and how do you trust your instincts about who to approach or allow into your life. How can you separate out your desires, your illusions, your loneliness and your replacement needs from your true wants for friendships. How do you keep control of your socializing and not let it become a way to mask and hide your grief so you don't work on healing, so you just cover up the pain. How do we overcome gender-based social expectations in making friends and still stay comfortable and safe in our choices.

This next section contains parts of the process I went through in trying to find people to bring into my life to help fill the empty spaces and also learn to live again. Some of it was easy but most of it, for me, was difficult and painful until I learned what I needed to know to move forward. And again, this is just what I experienced, it isn't meant to be what everyone needs or goes through. Please use what you can if it sounds reasonable, helpful or familiar to you.

Some places/ways I thought of that I might be able to meet people:

- Neighbors/friends of neighbors.
- Support groups/social opportunities associated with these groups.
- Social, topic or interest driven meetup groups.
- Gyms/yoga classes/senior centers.
- Restaurants.
- Bars, clubs, coffee houses.
- Places of worship.
- Local social media support groups

I actually tried most of these places over a couple of years and each one had its own challenges, ways of interacting, successes and rewards as well as failures. It is something some of us may have to try at some point if we need to find new people in our lives. We all need to find our own way to explore the possibilities that are available and to safely navigate the social requirements and patterns in each of the modalities we investigate.

I can't tell anyone how to do it, just that it turned out to be a very important growth area for me. Learning it was a major and critical part of much of who and what I have become, what I've done during my grief journey and was seminal in bringing me to a place where I could think about reasons for writing this book.

It seems to me that the process each of us follows towards finding and making friends depends on a large number of factors in each of our individual lives. Where we live, what we have access to, our age, our gender, our personalities and more, can all play a role here. For many of the people I've talked to, going out alone as an older adult, can be an almost insurmountable challenge that has not only social but also safety implications it would be well to consider.

Here's something I learned in my adventures of going out alone that evolved from a restaurant experience and then to a great realization one night in a wine bar…

I didn't begin my adventures by having a problem going to a restaurant alone. It was fairly easy for me, as an older man, to just go and find a table, bring a book, order dinner and read while I ate, finish and go home. I really never thought about doing anything different and the only interactions of the evening were talking to the server. It was really just about the food.

I was told about a local wine bar one day and I eventually convinced myself to go and check it out. So I finally went, by myself, and followed the model from the restaurant. I sat at a table, ordered wine and a cheese board and read my book and drank my wine and made small comments to the server/bartender whenever he came to the table. It wasn't bad, I liked the wine and the cheese so I decided I could come back another time.

Next time I came in, since I had already met the bartender, he motioned me to come sit at the bar. I sat down there and ordered my wine and cheese but this time, since he was being conversational, I didn't take out my book, I just sat, enjoyed the wine and food and amazingly, had a conversation with a person I barely knew.

It was a revelation to me, although I know it isn't that strange to many people. I realized by the end of the evening, which I enjoyed quite a lot, that when I went and sat at a table by myself with a book, I was essentially putting up a sign that said " I'm alone, don't bother me." By sitting at the bar, it appeared that not only the bartender but most of the other people sitting there, singles, couples and groups, were sitting there because they wanted to talk to people as well.

Amazing!

From that point onward, every restaurant and bar I went to, if I could, I sat at the bar and went about learning and practicing to be social, to be friendly to strangers and to relax into the social situation and just enjoy the conversation. It actually wasn't long before I learned enough to talk to most of the people I encountered in those situations. I also learned to leave people alone if they weren't into talking to me.

I realize this may be very obvious to many people but to me it was, as I say, a revelation and the beginning of a whole new chapter in my grief journey; the beginning of gaining the skills I needed to make friends and to understand how to become a friend as well.

It wasn't that I never had friends before, it was just that those past friendships had evolved more slowly and organically at school or work and without much conscious effort, so this was a whole different trip. It had also been over 30 years since I had to do anything like that alone and I had pretty much forgotten how I might have done it anyway.

I realize that for many people, going out alone and meeting people in public places can be a very socially difficult thing to do. In many of our lives, once we became part of a couple, going out was almost always done as a couple and relearning to do it alone, if we ever knew how to do it as a single, is often pretty difficult to consider. I also learned from talking to others that for many people who had to travel for work, going to a restaurant or bar alone while they were on the road was fairly common.

Finally, for many women, it simply wasn't and isn't ever done. Being alone in a bar or restaurant sent signals of intent or situation that were either incorrect or again, not welcome and something socially, never to be done. It was and is, in many ways, an invite to attention that could become unwanted and so best avoided. And I have to add as a safety issue, for women going out alone, even in apparently safe places, there is the potential of meeting people who have unwanted and possibly dangerous intentions.

So here again it's the unanswerable. There just isn't a right answer or a single answer that fits everyone and it's not all or nothing either. It's another place each of us needs to think about and find our comfort zone and then proceed slowly and carefully in what ever direction we want to explore.

I also should say that even having one other person going along on an outing changes the dynamics completely, so if going alone is not something you are comfortable with, consider adding at least one other person and see how that changes things.

What I know from all my investigations, from the social groups and my solo adventures to the restaurants and bars is that there was and is a real need in myself and in most of the bereaved spouses and partners I've talked to, to be social. If we are feeling isolated in and by our grief, we need to discover comfortable ways to get together and perhaps establish a (new) group of people to talk to and do things with to help fill the large amount of lonely time we now have to fill. To fill our needs for interaction and connections and even over time to add hugs, and especially, to build friendships.

Social Groups:

There is one modality that I want to support and talk about here and it is something I and a group of bereaved spouses and partners have been building and sharing for a number of years. It is an easy way to meet people that is mostly safe and controlled as well. This is how it evolved and where it's taken us.

The local hospice that helped us through the final days of Andi's illness also had a very well organized and wide ranging set of grief programs, including individual counseling and support groups for various grief situations. I began attending their bereavement support group for spouses and partners about a month into my bereavement.

I went very hesitatingly, not expecting much but feeling I had better try something to help me to not feel like I was so alone or that I was going crazy with all the things going through my mind. It also was part of my search for friendships in the isolation of my situation.

In the end, that support group turned out to be one of the very important parts of my grief journey. I heard a lot of things I needed to hear and because the group was made up of people in all stages of their own grief journeys, I got many different perspectives along the time line of grief to think about and use to help me grow and learn.

Our once-a-month meetings also gave me a sounding board for my own ideas and the things I was learning on my own and so there was a lot of validation and evaluation on my part in the weeks between meetings.

One of the more important parts for me was listening to some of the people who were further into their grief talking of how it had changed through time and that the intensity I was feeling was part of the "early grief" part of the journey and that there were other, less intense parts of the journey ahead that would not be nearly so debilitating as the early parts.

Much of what I'm writing about in this book has its roots and its origins in those meetings. Many of the topics from the meetings are mirrored here and I am grateful for the model they provided for my thinking during my bereavement and in the creation of this project.

Near the end of my first year of attending the support group, someone suggested that we try to begin getting together outside of the formal meetings and have a potluck at people's houses once each month. Most of those who got together wanted (and needed) something more than the once-a-month meetings of the support group to help our healing and growth.

It was another questionable start for me, I wasn't sure I was ready to socialize like that when I wasn't sure I knew how to talk to new people in my life and I was still crying uncontrollably every time the waves hit me, but I agreed to participate.

For the next year, one Sunday a month, we found someone willing to host and then we would gather at their house and spend a couple of hours eating and talking and getting to know each other. We had lots of tissues and lots of hugs for when anyone got caught up in their grief and needed some comfort and through it all, we learned that sharing our grief and being with people who understood what we were going through, who "got it," was a very healing activity.

And an unexpected consequence of the process of both the support group and the potlucks was that we were becoming what I've come to think of as "friends in grief."

In the normal course of our lives we often take many months and years in the making of friends in the various places we meet people. It takes time in the short conversations we usually share to build commonality and shared experiences and open up about our lives, thoughts and feelings until, gradually, we become friends.

In our support group sessions, however, we often quickly began to share very deep and personal and often intense parts of ourselves. Through that process, we learned in a relatively short time a lot about each other, and we compressed perhaps years of getting to know one another into that time as well.

And surprisingly to me, when we started meeting in a social environment, the pathway to friendship was accelerated by both our common grief experiences and by the opening up we had done and experienced in the support group. I expect there was also a very strong need for friends in all of us if old relationships and friendships began to slip away for all the reasons I've written about earlier.

Within a year or so, what began as a small group of 6-7 people began to grow as we invited more and more people to join us to expand beyond the support group experience. The group has grown to as many as 30 people at times and before we became unable to gather in person during the pandemic, we ended up moving our potlucks to a local wine bar that allowed us to take over their space one Sunday a month.

From talking to people in the group and from my own feelings, it appears that the socialization of these get togethers has been in its own way as large a part of our later healing as the support group was in the early parts. It has been a very definite growth and moving forward for all of us who continue to meet every month.

And it turned out that wasn't all of it. After a while, we tried going out as a group to not only the wine bar, but also to a restaurant in the evenings during the week. We tried to pick places that were quiet enough so that we would still be able to visit and talk. It began as a one-evening-a-month event and then before the pandemic stopped us, it became two evenings a month and then, it became every week.

After we stopped meeting during the pandemic, we tried to stay connected by doing an online meeting for Friday happy hour each week, and that worked well but obviously wasn't as nice as our face-to-face get togethers had been. Once things opened up again, the group decided to start meeting at outdoor locations and it was a much smaller group for a while since not everyone was comfortable meeting yet.

It took over a year but we grew back to having 20-25 people each time we met and it moved back to the every week get togethers at different locations around town. We also continued to have potlucks periodically to share food and conversation.

I highly recommend that anyone who is part of any type of bereavement group try to duplicate our successful move to socialization and out of the isolation that grief almost always brings us. The hardest part at the start seems to be finding someone who wants to organize, coordinate and gather a group together.

I found though, that once we had a list of people and their email contacts created, it got much easier; the hardest part then was finding people to host each month without imposing on the same one or two people each time. As long as everyone was willing to take their turn, I found it to be very doable. And the move to public venues that were quiet enough for us to gather and talk each week has become even more successful in adding more social possibilities beyond the potlucks.

During the writing of this chapter a new evolution of our social groups began. At some point during the previous few months I had begun to realize that there were not just friendships forming within the group, but there were also relationships beginning to grow. There were couples forming. There were even two people who announced that they were going to get married. Well, how lovely that was since that was the point of getting together in our groups in the first place... Wasn't it?

But while I was really happy for the couples and happy that they had found ways of healing and working through their grieving, I was a little uncomfortable though, when I noticed that some of the most recent people to join the group, many of whom were fairly newly bereaved and pretty raw emotionally, were looking at the couples and the affection they were displaying and it was not helping them to heal. Seeing the closeness and affection in those couples seemed to be making them uncomfortable and was actually triggering their grief and sadness.

I thought about it for a number of weeks without realizing just why it was making me uncomfortable until someone said, "but they aren't 'on their own' anymore so shouldn't they be leaving the group?"

That was it, it wasn't what the group was supposed to be about in my mind. I had expected when I began coordinating it, that as people healed over time, they would then leave the group and pursue life outside the group as they moved forward.

So it was confusing to me because not only had people in the group grown and done a large amount of healing, they had also created a group of friends and more, just as I hoped they would. What I didn't see in advance was that once they became friends and enjoyed getting together each week, that they wouldn't want to leave, they would just want to keep going and meeting and enjoying what we had built as the new lives they were living evolved.

So again, it worked. Everything I hoped that people would find in the group was happening. It was a great success and contained a lot of healing for a large number of people.

But, it really wasn't serving new people very well at all any more. There was a disconnect for them when they saw how close some of the people who had been in the group for a while had become. The new people weren't feeling as comfortable coming in as those of us who were there longer had felt when we were just starting the group, probably because we had no one in front of us who had already moved forward into relationships, to make us feel out of place.

So once I saw it clearly, the model had to change. I didn't think it was right or even possible to ask people to leave the group when they were no longer "on their own," although it was my first thought as I hung on to my original idea. Rather, I realized finally, that it would be much better to start a new group just for the newly bereaved.

The new group would be a place where it was once again only people in the first year or two of their journeys and who all had pretty similar needs, and where we could, in a way, start the socializing process again. We could begin slowly again, a once a month potluck, just so the socialization process could move at a slower pace for those who chose to participate, and they would now all be people who were in a fairly similar place in their grief journeys as well.

So now, instead of bringing people directly into the group of "old friends" that the original group has become, we have indeed started a new group and have started having potlucks. They are once more a place where new friendships are already beginning to find a place to grow. If any of those in the new group want more socialization, they can easily make their way to the original group's meetups and join in at whatever level they are comfortable with.

And yet again, it changed. Once we had the potluck group set up and people began to gather and interact, as it had for the first group, they began to not only enjoy the interactions but wanted to have more of them. As it had been for the members of the original social group, this group was reaching the end of what they were able to get from the once-a-month support group meetings they were attending. Many of them had cycled through most of the topics being discussed there and most didn't see that they would be gaining anything from visiting those places again.

So, at one of the potlucks, the group asked if we could maybe add another get together each month but this one would be a discussion group. One where we could talk about different topics that were now becoming important to them during the beginnings of their healing journeys. So using the format of my support group work, we began having a discussion group once a month as well.

And then, since I haven't learned nor want to say no, they asked to have yet another meeting to just allow them to talk together about what ever came up. So we agreed to a format of meeting for an open support group once a month as well.

And they decided to call the group the Phoenix Group as a place to help them to rise out of the ashes of their grief.

Interestingly, as it has expanded, the Phoenix Group hasn't become a social group. It has become a couple of grief discussion groups and a potluck each month. This particular group of people is interested in talking about grief and working towards healing more than in finding the social activities the earlier group found. No judgements here from me. I think both are and will be valuable. It's just turned out to be another way a group of bereaved spouses and partners can come together and help each other to find hope, healing and wellness.

Socializing:

Just a short general note here that socializing or the want to socialize, like so many other parts of our grief journeys, happens at a different point and at a different rate for each of us. We each probably come to a place when we feel the need to have other people in our lives, when we want some company and a chance to interact in our own time.

Most of the conversations I've had suggest that it is best to go slowly at first, to not immediately jump into "high intensity" situations like loud, couple-filled bars and clubs, or by joining singles meetup groups or using online dating apps. Although as always, if that's what you feel you want or need, perhaps because its something you remember from before you entered your marriage, then absolutely you can try it.

But going slowly and meeting people in a "low energy" situation and not in an emotionally charged environment seems to have a benefit of allowing you to talk and actually get to know and be around people for itself, for the social aspects of making new friends perhaps, and not as a "stay busy coverup" for your feelings of grief. Our social, potluck and discussion groups have bridged the gap between our isolation and finding a gentle way to edge back into socializing that I highly recommend and urge groups of like-minded bereaved spouses and partners to try to create in their communities.

Questions:

- Have you experienced old friends not wanting to interact with you as they used to? Can you see the reasons that might be happening?

- Can you think of some healthy ways to react and deal with those changes in old friends behaviors?

- How might you find safe ways to make new friends if you need to?

- Can you find others to join with and become friends with on your grief journey?

- Do you feel a need for socializing?

- Would you be willing to join a support group and any social aspects of that group?

- Would you be willing to initiate support or social activities for yourself and other bereaved spouses and partners in your community if there are none available?

Chapter 13

Semantics, Emotions and Acceptance

Early in our grief journeys, I've seen that we are often "controlled" by our grief. What we experience seems to mostly be coming from our emotional-self and rarely has much of our rational-self involved. Thoughts, feelings and emotions just cascade over and through us and mostly all we can do is "ride the wave" as best we can, let the current carry us where it will until "the tide turns" and we can begin to find ways to re-engage some active control in our lives and move towards the shore of hope and healing.

Since we really don't want it to continue and since we won't always be actively and painfully grieving, as I wrote about in Chapter 7, when we are ready, we may want to begin to investigate and initiate ways to take an active part in our reconstructive process.

I think it's important as we begin the process of actively addressing our reconstruction, to remember that grief is a complex of a wide range of feelings, emotions and thoughts.

So, this chapter is about trying to identify some of the emotions contained within our grief and about the semantics of it; what do the words we use to talk or think about our grief actually mean and describe?

As I was working though my early grief, particularly during the first year, I found that the words I used to describe my thoughts, feelings and emotions needed to be as accurate as I could make them; for example, the sadness and the loneliness parts of grief are different things, they feel different and they need to be addressed differently because they each need different resolutions.

I remember one day during my first year, I was taking a walk and just thinking about how I felt. It was one of those deep-grief days when I felt terrible all over, mentally, emotionally and physically and nothing felt right. I started to think that I would really like to not be feeling or continuing to feel this way. I kept asking myself what can I do to make it stop or go away. In some ways, this was the beginning of my active reconstruction period.

As is usual for me, I had to ask myself just what was I feeling and how had I dealt with something like these feelings in the past. At first I thought it was sadness that I was feeling and then I thought it was loneliness that I was feeling and then, well, I thought it must be grief I'm feeling and then I finally realized it was kind of a wash of all these emotions and more, all together and all coming at me from my emotions and my mind at the same time.

Then I thought that when I wanted to stop feeling sad in the past, I had to do certain things, I had to think certain things, do certain acts. Here's the interesting part to me, those things would be very different if, for instance I wanted to stop being lonely or angry or any other emotion.

What I learned after thinking about it for a while was: it's pretty important to know what you are talking about, what you are thinking about, what you are trying to work on and what you are trying to fix or change.

Because, if I'm trying to stop feeling sad, and I start doing the things that make me not feel lonely, then I don't fix the problem, I don't fix sad because I'm working on the wrong thing! I can't fix sad if I'm working on lonely!

Again, I also came to see that grief is actually not a single feeling and emotion by itself. When we are grieving, there are components of a large number of emotions present, usually at the same time. Our grief is a composite of all these things.

To illustrate that point, a friend shared a list of some emotions that might be involved in grief with me. Some of the things on the list included: shock, numbness, sadness, anger, guilt, regret, anxiety, loneliness, longing, yearning, resentment, fear, insecurity, helplessness and unfortunately, many more...

As we begin to try to sort it out for ourselves, as we tease it apart in our thoughts and try to see how we can make it better or at least make it hurt less, as we start on our reconstruction journey of hope and healing, I believe it's important to try to identify what we are dealing with and working on at any given time. Trying to solve the wrong problem leads to frustration and confusion and thoughts of "it's just not working and I don't know why..."

For me, from that time onward, I've gradually tried to learn to identify which parts of my grief I'm thinking about and working on as closely as possible so I could work on them in a way that actually led to some level of healing and resolution. I'm always trying to identify as clearly as I can what it is I'm trying to do and it has consistently helped me to better find the healing I'm looking for.

Smoke screen actions and reactions, what's really going on here?

Something Andi and I learned many years ago as we were building our lives together was that sometimes, expressions of annoyance or even anger, especially as arguments that were difficult to resolve, were what we ended up calling "smoke screens." The external expression of annoyance or anger between us was sometimes not about what we were expressing in our anger or arguing about at all. In those instances, although we seemed to be arguing about the thing that set us off or kept us arguing, the real issue was often something completely different.

It was often something that had been hidden inside, something not expressed or acknowledged that was building up and that was what was really bothering us and really why we were arguing. The actual trigger event and what we thought we were arguing about was not really the important part of what was going on at all.

We called these things "smoke screens" because they were hiding the real issues. If we became angry with each other and started going at it about some seemingly minor problem, when it didn't seem like we were getting anywhere, when we weren't finding resolution, one of us would finally ask, "what's the real issue here? What is this anger a smoke screen for? Can we stop arguing and find out what it is that we are really angry about and work to resolve that instead of going on about and not resolving this much less important thing we are superficially angry about?"

This almost always led us to taking the time and finding the real issues and because we had stepped away from the anger, we could open up and talk much more reasonably about what was really bothering us and that made it so much easier to find real resolution and move on.

With that to set the stage, lets talk about... Anger! Experiencing, expressing and dealing with anger during our grieving, especially when anger can also be a smoke screen in its own way for a frustrated lack of control, fear or pain, is something I think is helpful for us to address as we work through our grief.

Not everyone feels or expresses anger in grief. Not everyone has issues with anger even if they do feel some of it while dealing with their often very fragile emotions when they are grieving. If we do feel any of these things and because they can come and go and can sometimes show up when least expected, I've included this discussion here to explore.

I didn't really think that I experienced a lot of anger that I expressed or recognized during my grief. While writing this, however, I did remember some things that happened that were probably smoke screens and now make me believe I was indeed holding some anger inside without realizing it in the early parts of my journey.

But, I have heard many people talking strongly about their anger in the support group meetings I've attended and in conversation with other bereaved spouses and partners over the years, so I'm guessing that it is probably there at some level in most of us. And we probably really do have things we feel angry about considering what has happened to our lives and our loved ones.

There can often be a lot of lack of control involved in bereavement and lots of unresolved questions we may be asking like: "Why? Why me? Why you? Why now? This is so unfair. Why did you let this happen? How am I going to go on? Why did you leave me here alone? How can I deal with all this? Why did you say that? Why don't you understand?" And many other questions like these.

These things can lead us to frustration and pain and that can sometimes turn into anger. They can sometimes make us want to verbally or even physically act out or even strike out in some way to release some of our frustration at what has happened to us and to our loved ones and to our lives and futures.

As I'm writing this in early 2022, anger has been more frequently showing up in my support group meetings. It is mostly from people who have lost a spouse or partner (or other loved one) during the COVID pandemic. Especially early in the pandemic, when things were very out of control around the world, many people were kept from visiting or even seeing their loved ones and were frequently unable to be with them at the end of their lives and so were unable to find any solace or closure. There is, to me, an understandable amount of anger in this community of the bereaved that I believe has yet to find resolution.

So back to anger:

People have talked to me about the frustration they feel associated with lack of control, of things happening that were outside their plans and certainly outside their ability to change or effect. They've talked about the loss of not only their spouses or partners but of the loss of the futures they had planned or expected.

Financial losses are another large change many have expressed anger about. Some talked about fear of what the future had to bring and how they would handle it alone. How could they make good decisions without having the shared decision-making process they had grown to depend on in their marriage?

The frustrations and lack of control we experience during our bereavement can not only be at the surface, they can also be submerged below our grief and below our conscious thoughts. As it can when we don't let ourselves express or acknowledge our grief, these feelings too may build up and grow inside of us without us being aware of it. Sometimes the first indication of their existence is when they break through to the surface and we find ourselves having an angry reaction to something seemingly not that important (a smoke screen?).

Anger, at ourselves or others, can sometimes be an important way to release some of the tension our frustration may cause. But when we turn it on ourselves or on things or people that only seem to be the cause, the anger may really be just a smoke screen. It can especially be a smoke screen for things we really can't do anything about but maybe are the real issue.

I believe that whenever possible, if we find ourselves getting angry, especially if it happens often, we should consider trying to stop and ask ourselves why we are angry, what is it about a situation, about something that happened or what some person said or did that makes us angry and more importantly, why does it make us feel that way?

If we can stop and think about why we are angry, often times we may find that our anger is indeed a smoke screen. We may find that we really weren't angry about the words someone said or what they did, we were actually angry because what someone said or did triggered our deeper feelings of lack of control, or feelings of grief and pain.

Maybe if we just lash out because we can't do anything about the real reasons, we are just "shooting from the hip" at a convenient target. Sometimes after the anger has passed, we may need to apologize to ourselves or to others for things we may have done or said and maybe try to explain what we learned from the outburst.

Can we find a way to not let those frustrations express as anger towards ourselves or someone or something else? Instead, can we try to learn what we can do to resolve the unresolved feelings within ourselves? Can we find ways to do this by ourselves or in conversation with others who understand our feelings or those who are trained to help us find solutions for these deep frustrations?

How might we do that?

Something to think about:

In grief, many of the things we are unhappy and frustrated about our inability to control or change, are just that. We can't do anything about them. They happened. They are unchangeable and nothing we can do will make it any different. They certainly include, in large part, whatever it was that happened to our loved ones that we couldn't stop or change or fix and of course, that our loved ones are not here with us any longer as well.

Some people have told me that they are actually angry with their loved ones for leaving them alone, for leaving them to do so many of the things their loved ones used to do or that they did together that they now have to learn to do on their own. That, by itself, is a pretty large package of possible frustrations to deal with, especially when they are loaded on top of all the other emotions our grief causes us to feel.

But it's also important, at least intellectually to start with, to remember that for many of these things, no one is or was responsible. No one may have caused these things to happen. We may not have been able to do anything to keep them from happening. For many of them, that's just how it was. And somehow, we have to try to find a way to fight any feelings of hopelessness and pointlessness this may create within us and learn to live with that too. These are some of the most difficult things we need to come to see, learn and accept in our healing and growth as we move forward.

Obviously, some things that happen in our lives are caused by others. Some things were indeed done by other people and we do have good reasons for our anger. It is sometimes hard, especially during our grieving, to separate our justifiable anger for wrongs done from the frustrated anger that comes from our lack of control and the loss of our loved ones and our futures.

The anger I am trying to address here is the anger we direct towards ourselves and/or other people or towards our loved ones or even towards God because of things that happened that were indeed out of our control but that were no one's fault. Seeing those distinctions clearly and not taking our frustrations out as anger at or on ourselves or others, of not assigning blame when there was no blame either to ourselves or others, is often another very challenging but important part of our healing and of learning to live within and beyond our grief.

What did you learn from that?

I read in an autobiography by Carlos Santana (The Universal Tone) that one of his friends and fellow musicians would often say "what did you learn from that" whenever anyone would get angry and lose their temper and go off on someone. I like that idea, it has such a sobering feeling to it. It changes the tone of the moment and makes a person think instead of emotionally striking out or arguing back.

It seems like a very powerful way to get to the core of what we are angry about in ourselves and to look more closely and deeply at the reasons for our anger and in my terms, to see if the anger is a smoke screen for something else. It is also a way to perhaps not let our anger turn outward that way in the future.

If we can take the time to figure out why we are angry, before or after the fact, maybe we can find things we can work on over time to address the actual causes of that anger. Maybe we can find things to change in ourselves that address the reasons we are angry.

I remember a night at a support group meeting when I told the counselor that I was angry about something someone had said and how they were acting. The counselor looked at me and replied, "What does that say about you! What about or within you is getting angry at someone being and expressing themselves."

Sure made me stop and think!

Acceptance: Dealing with the things we can't change...

A core part of surrender, and of reaching healing and wellness is acceptance. I believe that one of the most difficult but also one of the most important parts of the healing process is finding acceptance of our new reality.

Coming to gradually and slowly understand that our loved ones are not coming home, that the place they occupied in our material and emotional lives is going to be empty of them forever and nothing we do or wish or think is going to change that is a very difficult thing to do. It can often take years for it to gradually come into focus in our minds and emotions.

Coming to accept that reality is perhaps one of the hardest and most painful things we are faced with doing during our healing journeys. There is often anger, regret, guilt, sadness and probably most of the other emotions that live within grief that we experience and have to work through along the way.

But acceptance is almost essential to building our new lives, to start to look for and find ways of thinking, of acting and of living that both honor what was and create what will be as we transition from us, to me living and being here alone. Until we accept what has happened, it is difficult to want to even begin to look for alternatives isn't it?

Denial can also be a part of the process of reaching or not reaching acceptance. The magnitude of all we are experiencing is so very difficult to believe and come to terms with that sometimes it's easier to deny it and keep the hope alive in our hearts that we may yet somehow see things turn around and we will have our loved ones back in our lives again.

I know I kept saying early in my journey as I tried to convince myself to move forward, "having Andi back is the one thing I want most in the world and it's the one thing I can't have. So what do I do now?" I still say that from time to time…

Acceptance also doesn't seem to be a linear process, nor does it usually come in one single flash of insight or light. It seems to grow gradually within us over time as it slowly comes into focus. It can also move like our grief does, sometimes we go forward and think we've got it and sometimes we go backwards and don't have it and sometimes we stagnate and don't seem to be going anywhere at all.

These are all part of the process and kind of a "normal" way for us to learn to accommodate the huge changes that have occurred in our lives.

This is only how it happened to me, but acceptance seems to have crept up on me almost without my knowing it. I wrote these lines in a song sometime in the third year of my bereavement and it strikes me as I'm writing this, that there was a measure of acceptance here about what had happened and that my realizing it by putting it in the song had definitely helped to allow me to move forward in my life.

"I know you are at peace now,
resting softly, out of pain.
You are done with all that sadness
and flying free again..."

From Phoenix Moment... (© Howard and Andrea Fischer 2020)

I know I realized when I was writing it that I wouldn't have wanted Andi to go through one more moment of the pain she was enduring and so I had to let her go. But it took some time for me to accept that not only had her spirit truly moved on but that it actually, for her, was a good thing. I think when I begin to understand and accept that, it helped me to find a more peaceful acceptance of almost everything else going forward.

I do know that not everyone's situation had this aspect in it but I believe that it shows that no matter what our particular story is, we will eventually come to find a place when we understand and accept the deep realities of what has happened.

In addition to the largest piece of accepting that our loved ones are not coming home, there are lots of other places and things we need to find acceptance of in this new reality. They are not always negative things either. Although it may be hard to see them early on, there are also many potentially positive things in our journeys that we will come to accept as well.

A maybe "too long" list of things to consider that we may have to come to accept in our new lives:

- Being alone.
- Living alone.
- Having to do everything our spouse used to do.
- Figuring out what to change, keep or leave out in our new lives.
- Taking care of all the material world responsibilities by ourselves.
- Making decisions alone.
- Traveling alone.
- Dealing with medical issues alone.
- Dealing with loneliness.
- Dealing with sadness.
- Dealing with finance changes or issues alone.
- Dealing with living arrangement changes.
- Losing old friends.
- Knowing what to do if family and/or friends don't know what to say or avoid us.
- Having no one to talk to, especially in the evenings.
- I can't sleep!
- My mind keeps racing and looping.
- I can't stop crying.
- Needing to make new friends.
- Not knowing know how to make new friends.
- Enjoying being with/going out with my new friends.
- Feeling guilty for being with/going out with my new friends.
- Feeling guilty for changing things, for wanting to do things on my own.
- Knowing we have to move forward.
- Finding wellness.
- Being happy.
- Being ok.
- Having a good time.
- Coming to like living alone.
- Being "relieved" to not be a caregiver anymore.

- Feeling guilty about having any of these feelings.
- Learning how to not be a caregiver anymore.
- Taking care of and being gentle with ourselves.
- Learning to honor and remember our loved ones without grieving them.
- Realizing we are no longer actively grieving.
- Having to rebuild a new life.
- Learning that we are strong.
- Others?

Some things we may need to accept doing without (temporarily or forever):

- Affection in both physical and emotional ways.
- Affirmations.
- Someone to share the story of our day with.
- Someone to hold us when we are sad or need to cry.
- Someone to bitch to.
- Someone to sit quietly and just be together with.
- Someone to eat dinner with.
- Someone to go out with.
- Someone to do "nothing" with.
- Someone to rub our feet or whose feet we can rub.
- Your shared purpose in life.
- Your future plans.
- Others?

Again, once acceptance of any of these things begins to appear, there seem to be times when our acceptance is strong and healing and then, at other times, often unexpectedly, the reality of what has happened reaches out and grabs us again and the pain of that realization triggers our grief back into full intensity, hopefully and thankfully just for a short time and then that too passes.

As it is in so many parts of grief, I want to say here, yet again, that as I see it and have experienced it, there is no timetable to it. We each reach acceptance in our own time and in our own way and when it happens for us, that's when it happens.

I believe that it's not something we can or should anticipate either. Looking for it to happen, feeling we are somehow not healing properly if it hasn't happened, is a no-win situation full of little but frustration. Impatience is not usually a good strategy for dealing with our grief. We probably aren't going to get a quick fix!

That is one of the reasons I personally tried to stay away from expectations of what was going to or was supposed to happen based on anything anyone else had written, said or done. What I have learned and have tried to express throughout this book is that there really is no timetable. I believe that you are best served by dealing with what is happening as and when it occurs in your own life with few or no expectations of what it means or when it's "supposed to happen." I've seen during my own journey and with numerous other bereaved spouses and partners, that most often, the changes have been fairly slow to develop and many times I've only noticed them once they had passed.

Impatience:

Since I've mentioned impatience, I think it would be good to expand on that idea a bit more here. I've heard it expressed by people along the way that they were in a hurry to get through their grief and "get over it". They were tired of the pain and the inability to function as they might want to and they wanted to get through it, be done with it and leave it behind them as quickly as possible. They really didn't like the idea that they might have to feel that way for years!

In many ways, that's not surprising. Grief is usually such a long and difficult process and especially at the start, it is painful and debilitating and a lot of people will try to find various types of avoidance reactions trying to replace the grief.

So, I understand impatience, I get wanting to move forward quickly and not having to go through it any more. But, I also know, from my own journey and from numerous conversations and observations with other bereaved spouses and partners that it doesn't really work like that.

As I keep writing, everything in life happens when it happens and while we can work on things along the way, while we can try to learn and grow, we almost always experience things only when they come upon us. We can rarely make them happen any sooner than when they enter our lives.

The strategy that worked best for me was to do something about each thing as it happened to me. I slowly learned that usually, I couldn't make them happen in my time at all, all I could do was my best to deal with them in their time, when they showed up in my life and I had to deal with them.

Looking for positive and effective thoughts and solutions:

As a wrap for this chapter, I want to say that early in our bereavements not much looks positive, not many thoughts are uplifting and solutions of any sort seem almost impossible for us to find. As time passes, as the waves of grief become less strong and come less often, we slowly begin to assume some control of our lives again and with that, it is important to try to look for positive ways to cope with the many things that have changed in our lives.

I think it is also important and a very strong part of the healing process, to gradually begin to find ways to replace our sadness, our pain and our anger (and the myriad other emotions) with positive, forward-looking thoughts and ideas. I think that after the shock and deep emotional distress of our early grief, we eventually need to find and learn ways to reach a place of acceptance of what has happened so that we can begin to entertain new ways of thinking, living and moving forward in our lives.

Questions:

- Where are you at in the process of learning to accept what has happened?

- Is there an aspect of denial in your thinking?

- Can you identify what you are feeling angry about if you are feeling it?

- Can you see any smoke screens in your thinking?
- What coping skills, social skills and life skills do you think you might need to learn to deal with any anger you feel and to move forward in your life?

- How does acceptance affect your anger if you are feeling either or both?

- Are you feeling impatience? What are you impatient about in your grief journey?

Chapter 14

Learning to Become More

Honor your
Loved Ones
in all that you do
and all that you
become...

G *rief can make us feel less but it can also become an opportunity to become more:*

As we move forward and begin to find healing and wellness, our grief journeys can also become a time to learn and to grow if we let them. In a similar way, we can work to learn to find ways to look at the memories of our loved ones and our lives together without the filter of our grief coloring everything and we can come to remember and celebrate our lives together as they were.

Two possibilities I want to start with before I write about growing and becoming more are: first, finding ourselves "stuck" on plateaus during our grief journey and second, perhaps having our grief turn into a habitual way of thinking that may slow or stop our movements forward toward hope, healing and wellness.

Getting stuck on a plateau:

As I've written about before, our grief feelings and responses will change through time as the intensity, frequency and height of the grief waves change. Usually the waves become less intense and come less often but sometimes, we may find that we get temporarily stuck along the way.

Getting stuck is actually a fairly common thing I've encountered in talking to other bereaved spouses and partners. Sometimes, especially early in our bereavement for a time, there may seem to be no change in the intensity of our grief at all. Sometimes, for no apparent reason, after a period of growth, there is a period of seeming stagnation.

When we seem to get stuck or to not grow or change for a while and especially if it goes on for too long, we may become frustrated by having the same feelings, the same level of grieving day after day. We may become fearful that something has gone wrong, that we have somehow done or thought something to derail our healing. We may become sure something is wrong when we lose our forward momentum and perhaps revert to earlier places in our grief and maybe even become fairly trapped by inertia once again.

On a more positive note, perhaps if we can recognize the plateaus and realize that they are usually temporary parts of the process, we can learn to wait them out, do our best to stay positive through them and then move on when it's time to do so.

We can also perhaps choose to begin to learn new things, especially during those plateau times and by doing so move ourselves and our grief journey into other channels of thinking and move off of the worn pathways our grieving has fallen into and began to chart new directions.

Here again, it seems to be pretty individual. How long a plateau lasts, how often it happens, if it happens at all, what we do about it, all these seem to affect each of us differently.

The important thing here I believe, is to know that these "plateaus" in our bereavement are usually temporary stops along the road. They don't last forever and they may even be an essential part of the healing process, a time when we think about and digest what we have learned and felt up to that point until we are ready to move forward again. Then, when we reach a place where we can move forward, we will.

Falling into habits of grief:

The second possibility is that through time, doing and thinking many of the same things our grieving brings to our minds and emotions repeatedly, having the same patterns of thought, feeling and action over and over may bring us to a sort of "Ground Hog Day" of what I think of as habits of grief.

The circular and repetitive thoughts that often lodge in our thinking early in our grief journeys when we have the least ability to effect them, can become almost normal ways of thinking and even become ways of life later in our journey. The longer we stay in one pattern, the deeper the channels can become and the more difficult it can become to change them. In a sense, by the repetition, we are establishing habits of grief.

These are not the routines or rituals I've written about earlier. Those tend to be healthy habits we purposely create to guide us in our healing journeys. The thoughts and actions I am looking at here are more the circular, repetitive patterns of thinking and perhaps unhealthy thoughts and actions, the what if's or regrets, that our grief has imposed on us and that we can fall into and remain locked into over time.

I've also talked to people who not only seemed like they are locked into a pattern but that pattern looked to me like they had become almost "addicted" to their grief, especially those who seemed to be getting a lot of attention and sympathy from others by using their grief, pain and sadness, consciously or unconsciously, to gain that attention.

At some point, I believe it is important to learn to find ways to stop the more negative and unhealthy repetitions and patterns of our grieving. I think it's very important to begin to learn new ways of thinking and looking at life to replace those patterns. As we substitute the new for the old, we then become actively engaged in the process of healing and building our (new) lives toward wellness.

Finally, I need to say, that if you are especially frustrated with being on one of the plateaus or by being stuck in a repetitive pattern, if it goes on way longer than you feel it should and especially if it makes you feel worse than you were before when it doesn't get any better, those are times, I believe, that it would be good to talk either with others who have shared the grief experience in a support group or with a friend you can trust.

If you feel that you are not able to handle it in those ways, it would be good to seek out a professional counselor to help guide you through to the understanding it takes to move to the next stage of your growth and healing.

Onward to becoming more!

❀

Mental, social and spiritual gardening:

A wonderful idea I got from the Carlos Santana autobiography (The Universal Tone), was that of "spiritual gardening." This idea contains the possibility of working on ourselves, of growing spiritually and emotionally as well as intellectually. It's about taking the time to "pull the weeds, to fertilize and water" new ideas, skills and emotions and in the context of this book, to find ways to use our bereavement as a tool for improving our lives and ourselves.

Here's what I want to consider for the rest of this chapter: While grief can often make us feel less, can our grief also be a time to learn to become more? Can it be a time when we open the door to intentional change in our lives and if we want to, a time to examine ourselves and decide what we want to do or be next? We have the time!

In the empty spaces of our grief, while we can't replace what is no longer there, maybe we can fill that space with soil, fertilize it and water it and where the garden of our love grew, we can grow a new garden, a different one, not a replacement but still one that is full of love and honor and memory as well as growth, healing and life.

And we can also pull some weeds from our own garden-of-self, water and fertilize here too and find new things to grow in our social, mental and emotional life to make us better and help us to actively live again.

While our grief is one of the most painful and disorienting times in our lives, because we have had all of our certainties and sure of's thrown to the wind, as we try to rebuild, we also have the opportunity to work on things, to perhaps become better people, to take more time "working on ourselves" than we have ever been able to do or wanted to do before.

The empty moments, the time we no longer fill being with our spouses or partners can seem to diminish us but it can also be a gift, once we are ready to accept it, that we can use to grow in, to learn in, to change in and especially to find ways to honor our loved ones in by becoming more.

What types of things might we do? What things can we focus on or work on that might be places for growth and learning? What can you think of that you might do to fill the time you now have available that you might not have been able to do earlier in your life? How might you honor your loved one with new or expanded things you do as you build your new life?

Learning anything helps you focus and grow:

In the first month of my bereavement, I was given the opportunity to meet with Beth, a music therapist associated with the support group I was attending. I have always played guitar but during the last few years of Andi's illness, I was just too tired and probably too sad inside to pick it up and play. When I told Beth I played, she suggested bringing guitars to one of our meetings and we could play together and see what happened.

At our next meeting, we were going to play some music. We started by talking, mostly me telling my story and expressing my grief but finally I got out my guitar and we tried to find some common music we could play together. What I found was that after not playing for a few years, I couldn't really play much at all, nothing came out of it except frustration and another sadness added to my grieving.

I think I must have been fairly embarrassed and feeling sorry for myself because Beth finally turned to me at the end of the session and basically told me that "if I wanted to say I was a guitar player I had to actually play guitar. What I was now was someone who used to play guitar!"

Kind of freaked me out. She went on to say, "if you want to say you play then you had better go and do it, start playing and when you learn it again, then you can tell me you play guitar." And then she left, the session was over!

Wow!

After I stopped feeling sorry for myself, I realized that it was one of the most profound things I had ever been told and I treasure the honesty and the directness and I believe it changed me forever. I will always be thankful and grateful to her for what she gave me that day.

I picked up my guitar that evening and began to play. I have played almost every day from that day onward. I played till my fingers were sore, until I couldn't play another chord, and finally, after I got to a place where I could again play most of what I used to be able to play, I treated myself and bought myself a pretty nice new guitar and continued playing every day. I still play every day.

I have learned an enormous amount since that time, I can play for hours now and it has become one of the great treasures in my life. It has filled my evenings with music and a feeling of closeness with Andi that we are sharing in the music which I believe is always a connection to spirit. And in the end, what it took to get started and get to where I am now, was playing the first notes, playing again the next day and every day thereafter and letting the music take me away! Along the way, I also learned to sing! More on the music and where it has led us are in Chapters 3 and 6.

After about a year of playing, I was introduced to the idea of recording my music by my brother. He convinced me to get a digital recording program on my computer and sent me a digital converter that plugged into my guitar and let me make a digital file of the music.

All of this was totally new to me. Who knew you could do that...I started by buying a book on digital recording and how to use the computer program to record and spent the next year learning how to do it. It was mentally the hardest thing I had done in a very long time.

I struggled with new concepts and new ways to manipulate the data, I learned how to not just record but how to mix and modify the sound, to add more layers to the sound and ultimately how to take the finished project and make it into a file that could be listened to on my computer or my phone.

The big lesson to me from all of this is that learning anything requires my full attention. My focus while trying to first learn and then become proficient in both guitar and recording helped me to learn to concentrate again, to grow and keep my mind active and it took me out of my grief for those parts of the day I spent in the learning process.

Here's another lesson I learned many years ago but very much needed to relearn. One-pointedness, the total focus on a task is a form of meditation. It is a calming and elevating experience. If you are totally focused, you are also totally present, you are in the moment.

We often talk about this idea as mindfulness and especially in a grief situation, our focus on a task puts us in the present and not in the past. In our time of focusing our minds, hands, eyes and ears on a task, we are not actively grieving, we are totally present and for that time, leave our grief behind.

Of course, grief comes back. We go back to it when we stop focusing but the relief, the time away from active grief turned out for me to be a time of healing and growth. It is also a very powerful way to keep our minds active, to keep them flexible and not let them atrophy. It is very important to keep ourselves mentally healthy and mentally active as we grow older and grief for older adults can add a layer of stagnation to our thinking that works against our mental flexibility and abilities.

In some ways, that time of learning for me has had the bonus effect of making my thinking more clear than its been in a long time. I feel more able to learn, my memory is really better than ever and I believe that the learning and the focus are the keys to having rejuvenated my thinking and my ability to continue to grow and expand my understanding of so many things. It seems to have been a critical part of moving me towards healing and finding ways to create a new life for myself in 'the wake of the flood."

I read a line in a novel that said "once you stop learning, your life becomes so much less than it could be." I took that as a very clear message and one that my own experience has proven to me over and over.

What can you think of to learn now that you might not have had the time to do in the past? What new or interesting things might you want to explore in the time you have available now, perhaps something you always wanted to do that you never got the chance to try: learn a language, learn a new skill, learn an instrument, learn to cook, learn a craft or start a collection, writing, journaling, taking a class in something.

You can teach an old dog new tricks!

Re-discovering old hobbies:

Besides finding something new to learn, re-finding old hobbies, skills and abilities was another important learning experience for me in its own right. Since there was now a huge amount of time in my life, I needed to fill it with things to do once I began to overcome the early inertia and actually wanted to get off the couch and do stuff. I spent a lot of time soul-searching and self-questioning, trying to find things I might like to do and remembering what I had enjoyed earlier in my life that I might bring back into it and enjoy doing now.

I knew I wasn't going to go back to "partying" but I realized that there were a few things I had done that were hobbies over the years that I would have liked to have spent more time doing in the past but that I had stopped doing for any number of reasons. But in thinking about them, I realized I still liked the idea of doing them and though I had put them on hold, I imagined that the skills would return if I started doing them again.

I gradually added each one of those hobbies back into my life. While there was indeed a re-learning curve and it took some time to get my coordination and skill level back to where it had been, to where it allowed me to enjoy the hobby again, I was eventually able to let them all resurface and let them help to fill some of the lonely time that I now sadly had an abundance of.

Those hobbies still remain with me. Sometimes one or another of them becomes dominant and I spend a lot of time on it. Sometimes I put it down for a while and let another of them fill a lot of my time but at least one of them is with me most of the time. They have become a large and satisfying part of my life now as well as a large part of my healing. Spending hours a day focused and one-pointed on doing something I enjoy and can get lost in is a very important part (still) of my growing towards healing and wellness.

Are there some hobbies or things you stopped doing over the years that might be interesting or fun to reintroduce into your lives?

Honoring our loved ones by trying to live with purpose and intent as we create our new lives:

What would our loved ones want us to do or be or work on in ourselves and our lives as we move forward? Can we honor our loved ones by giving them the gift of us making these changes in ourselves?

I've written about this before in Chapter 7 but it has been such an important component of my growth and healing that I feel I should expand upon it and include it here.

If we are going to grow and move forward in our lives, which at some point we all have to do, if we are going to change, then we also have an opportunity to do those things as an act of love. We can make those changes with purpose, we can choose to change in ways that honor our loved ones.

We can choose to work at growing in ways that are perhaps what our spouses or partners would have liked for us to have been or have done earlier in our lives and that perhaps circumstances did not allow us to do. We can also believe that they would be happy to see us do those things even now, especially if they are things we enjoy.

While we might wish we had done them earlier, that may not have been possible in the living of our daily, often very busy lives, but now, with all the time we have to fill, we can take the time to work on those things. As we do them, we also don't have to feel remorse for not having done them earlier, we can just make them a gift to honor our spouse or partner as we do them now.

We can also use those changes to honor the memory of our loved ones in our external dealings. As we learn to become more of what our loved ones would have wanted us to be and more of what we would wish to be as well, people we interact with can see those changes in us. Our changes can remind people of our love (and our loved ones) as we change and grow and act in new and more positive ways.

Making changes and not just talking about them. Fighting mental inertia (again):

It's usually pretty easy to think of things you want to do or be. Throughout my life, I have had "great ideas," made promises to myself, made "resolutions" and made plans to do things, to change things and to learn things. In the business of living however, many of them never got done, something came up or I just didn't have the will, or the time, or the resources to follow through or carry them out. In general, I think that's pretty common behavior for most people.

Partially because of my age and partially because of a promise that I made to myself and to Andi early in my bereavement, to become more, not less, I don't feel I have the luxury anymore to not follow through, to not live up to the mental promises I make and the intent I have. Since much of what I try to do is now to honor Andi, I also have the strong desire and commitment to make these things come into being to honor her.

A very important part of making changes in my life, of becoming better and more and of doing things to honor Andi, of doing things I know she would affirm, and also in doing things for my own purposes, is now following through.

If I let myself be mentally lazy, if I say I want to do something or change something, (and maybe more so in the mental and emotional sense than in the material sense) it is important that I overcome those feelings of inertia and go forward and make it happen, that I work on it and practice it and keep at it until I master it.

I wrote about this in Chapter 7 also, but here again, if I make a promise to Andi or to myself to change something, to learn something and to become better, especially in ways I may be sorry I didn't change earlier in my life, or if I want her forgiveness for something I might regret, I need to deserve that forgiveness and not just think the thought but also do the act. I need to become the change I promise and so honor and affirm our love and my willingness to actually become better or different and not just make noise about it. Not an easy task, but very well worth the do!

Turning grief into gold:

This idea, though it's near the end of the book, is one of the most important things I learned in the first year of my bereavement,; something that became a goal and a light that I could head towards within the fog of my grief.

One of the saddest and most difficult things that happened over and over in that first year was that all my memories of our life together were turned to sadness or at least looked at with sadness. They were all overlain by my grief. Looking toward the past, no matter what I thought about, it always made me sad or triggered my grief and caused me to cry and sent that wave crashing over me full of "missing you" in almost every instance.

This is a quote from my journal at that time in my bereavement:

"what i would like is for as the pain and the missing and the loneliness gradually get less over time, i would love it if the core of our love would take hold of everything and instead of it making me sad when I saw something that meant something special to us that the pain would transition into a celebration of our love and all those things would instead once again make me see our love and be happy for all the wonderful things we did and were and all that you gave me and left for me and the joy of the amazing love we created would slowly take the place of the pain and let me remember with joy and honor and happiness what we had and what we did and who we were and that i could go beyond the pain of loss and missing you and find my way to a place of acceptance and another level of love where my remembrance of our time together and the beautiful masterpiece of love we built will become my core reality and my core of feelings and be happy we were able to build such a love with the time we had together."

So I thought, "what if I could learn to turn grief into gold?"

What I realized was that if I could change that feeling, if I could find a way to not have the memories trigger my grief, I would be able to remember our life together as it had been. I would be able to think of Andi and remember the good times, the special moments and even the bad times, not with grief but as a memory of who and what we were. I could again think about her and our life with a smile, with joy and with gratefulness for the love we shared and all the things we had been and done, and not let our past and all it contained continue to be drowned in grief and sadness.

And over time it worked! I have come through now to a place where I have separated my past and my memories from my grief. I can think about Andi and our life and see it as I remember it and not through the filter of my grieving. The memories are no longer automatic triggers to sadness, my grief no longer shrouds the past. The memories have regained their richness and brightness and have indeed turned into gold. Now, by seeing the golden memories and the brightness of our life together, I can remember it as the beautiful life it was.

Affirmation and Approval:

Something I didn't know I was missing…

Affirmation or approval is a powerful need in most people throughout their lives. The need we have for someone to tell us things like: "well done," or "good job," "great idea," or "you look nice today" is strong in us and for some people it can even be a driving force.

In most marriages, it is often a powerful part of what we do for each other. It's part of our caring and our affection and why we become happy to be together. And it seems to me that whether it's out front and obvious or tucked away and hidden, there is a glow that comes over us when our loved one tells us these things.

It may be rare or it may be often but for me, it always made me feel good to hear or to know by words or actions or a special look that Andi thought I had done a good job at some task I had undertaken or something I had done or said, something that she liked and took the time to tell me so.

As I wrote about in Chapter 9, one of the things I experienced early in my bereavement was a fairly serious loss of self-confidence. I began to doubt myself and not trust my abilities, even in things I was fairly competent at. I know that part of it was something I've written about before, that I was reacting to my rather unreasonable thoughts that I should have been able to do something to prevent what happened to Andi or in some way have changed things and made them better.

As I was thinking about how unproductive those types of thoughts and feelings were, it occurred to me that I also was missing something else that had made me feel good about myself and that was the affirmations we shared and how often we made each other feel good with compliments and affectionate approval throughout our lives together. And I realized how important that part of our relationship and of our love that was.

And now it was gone!

That seemed to be one of the subtle but definitely large parts of the "missing you" and the emptiness that had become part of my life. It took a long time, years actually, before I was able to actually identify what it was that I was missing but once I did, it was an "Aha!" moment in a way. As I've come to investigate it in myself, I'm finding that although it was in many ways a fairly subtle component of our lives, it was also hugely important and it was now a much bigger part of the sadness and emptiness than I would have thought.

So I thought I would write about it and explore it and see what I could learn about it that might help me to find healing for this part of myself.

And here's a corollary to this that occurs to me as I write; how much of what I do now in my life is being done to find affirmation, to fill that need and gap in my life?

I have tried to fill my life and my time with helping others, of doing things to promote hope and healing in others and trying to make an impact that is positive and uplifting for others. So trying to be honest with myself here, I have to ask myself how much of what I do is also reflecting my own need to find affirmation, to have someone tell me "well done" again or thank me for something I did for them, how much is also about my own needs?

I'm not sure it matters really, it doesn't change what I'm doing or even really the main reasons why, but I just wonder if somewhere in the background, I'm still looking to fill that empty affirmation-place inside me.

✿

The Next-to-Last Story:

There is another, later part to the affirmation discussion I am reluctantly sharing because while it tied up some of the questions I was asking myself, it was also a very difficult time for me and exposed some fairly deep emotions and places within myself that I wasn't all that aware of. It also showed me how deeply empty those places really were.

It also was a very out-of-control time for a couple of months during which I had to look deeply at who I was and how I was going to go forward and at some very deep needs I found within myself during the self-examination that I had to do to resolve what had happened.

It also, however, brought me to a very important set of realizations and I believe it was perhaps a final piece in my healing journey and my movement to wellness and seemingly to the end of my grief journey.

Sometime early in the fifth year of my bereavement I met a young woman who had come to teach a yoga class I was attending when the usual instructor was out sick. I really liked the way she conducted the class and at the end I went over and started a conversation and with each word seemingly, the energy she was giving off or projecting resonated more and more strongly within me.

The words and ideas about yoga and meditation we shared in the conversation were very interesting to me and somehow we also began sharing life stories. At the end of the conversation, we shared a hug and it was like an electric shock passing through me and I just had to say something and surprisingly she had felt the same energy on her side of it.

I knew I had to talk to her again so I asked for her contact info just so she didn't walk away and I never got another chance to talk and let that connection and energy happen again.

She ended up teaching the class the following week and again, we talked and the hug at the end was as electric as it had been the first time.

In our conversations, we mostly talked about finding some ways for her to possibly develop some guided meditations for my bereavement group and for me to possibly do a recording of her playing the healing sound bowls that were a large part of her class.

I also have to say that the other person in the interaction did not know this following part of the story. It happened totally in my mind and was an illusion I created that I never got the chance to share and I'm not entirely sure I would have anyway, I'm not terribly proud of what I did in my grief and my imagination.

So, here's were it got difficult. I had not felt such a strong energy or attraction to anyone in a very long time. I had also felt a strong sadness in her, her story included her own losses, of a divorce, of lost love and a loss of direction in her spiritual life. My first reaction was just about helping her. I wanted to help her not be so sad and hurting. But unfortunately, in my head, all by myself, I changed that pure compassion and I imagined that not only could I help her but that we could somehow come together and heal each other.

For a number of reasons, although I tried to find a way for us to get together and talk again and get to know each other more, we were never able to find a time we were both free and the best we ever were able to do was have a video conference conversation for an hour or so one day to talk about how we might share her knowledge of meditation and my grief support group needs and try to plan a way to incorporate what she knew into what I was doing.

So, in my mind, again, instead of sticking to the honest intent of her helping me with my support group work and me somehow helping her through her sadness, I built a huge fantasy of some future where we could be together, where we could fill the needs I thought we each had and where I could find love and affection and affirmation in my life.

As it developed in my head, feeling those things and having those thoughts actually ended up showing me some pretty strong things I felt that I was missing in my life, that were the parts of me that were still unhealed and also that they were the things I very much thought I needed to find in my life at that time.

I spent almost a week looping those thoughts and having imaginary conversations with this person who I really didn't know at all. I built a huge world of illusion and a "what if" future of us being together and of us healing each other.

After about a week, I realized what I had been doing. I had taken a very real wish for sharing what we could share to help me in my support group work and my wanting to help her in some way and turned that pure intent and energy into a personal fantasy and illusion of some self-satisfying future, and maybe the worst part was that I let it get away from me.

I ended up having to spend most of the next two months trying to stop the loops and the imaginary conversations. In order to do that, I had to deeply examine why I was doing it and what about me was causing me to fly off into this illusion. What needs did I have that I was trying to project onto this person and expecting them to solve for me?

So what was I missing that caused me to do this? After two months of very serious, every day, almost constant thinking and hard work trying to stop the thought-loops in my mind, I learned some very important things about myself.

It also led me to a place in my bereavement that I didn't know about. One day in the middle of all of my self-examination, I suddenly and unexpectedly found myself once again crying in that deep, uncontrollable grief-mode I hadn't felt or experienced in a long time. It came as a surprise that I still missed our life together and the space Andi filled in my days and nights with a sadness, loneliness and longing that was every bit as strong and all encompassing as it was in the early days of my grieving.

So, at that point, I learned that I was still pretty lonely at some level and that I thought at first that I was lonely for someone to fill those empty material parts of my life. Most of the illusions I created, I think, were to fill that supposed need.

I learned just how very strongly I was still missing Andi in my material life, and the part that surprised me the most, though it probably shouldn't have, was that for the first time, I realized that, maybe most of all, I missed the affection and the affirmations that were such a strong and important part of our marriage and the way we expressed our love and that I thought we could never share again, no matter how Andi and I journeyed together in spirit.

Now it gets even more interesting to me. I've told the story of the love flowers that were Andi's gifts to me throughout the years of my grief journey. I've written about the confluences where things happened with perfect timing and I knew that it was Andi contacting me and sending me her love in new ways across the veil.

As I was working through all the illusions and coming to a place where I could let them go and see them as the desires and fantasies of really just wanting Andi back in my life that they were, I actually got a very powerful message from Andi.

Not sure why it took so long for me to understand it but what she told me was: "hey, you know those flowers and the other things you have loved so much when they happened that allowed you to realize that I was still part of your life, well, they are really all my affection and affirmation coming to you still, just in a different way. Instead of being material caresses, they are of spirit now but they are still the same thing, they are still me expressing how much I love you, you just have to learn to recognize them in this new way, as you recognized that they were messages from me in the first place."

Well, that sure changed everything. Once I had spent a few days digesting that, once I began to accept what I was "hearing," I began to realize that those things I thought I was missing in my life, the affirmations and the affections and even the caresses had also shifted into our spirit journey and where not missing at all, as with every other part of our spirit journey, I just had to learn to see them differently.

And over the next six months or so, as I came to see more and more clearly that it was true and that they were indeed happening and that they did indeed touch and fill those places in me that I thought were empty, the emptiness began to fill. Rather, my feeling that they were empty began to change and I learned and grew to feel complete again, in a different way and yet it was still the same. It was still us, together and still sharing all the parts of our love, just in a different way of sharing.

There's just one last piece I want to add. Recently, the person in the story ended up taking over teaching the yoga class I was attending when my original teacher moved on to another position at a different studio. So there she was back in my life.

We talked the first day she came in to teach the class and she actually remembered that I had offered to record one of her sound bowl sessions and she asked me if I was still interested and if so, would I do the recording during the next time she led one. I told her I would since I had really wanted to do it in the first place, and during the few weeks before the class, I decided I needed to tell her the story of what had happened, to tell her about all the fantasies I'd created and what the entire experience had meant to me. I also needed to let her know that, without mentioning her name, I was going to tell the story in my book as well.

So on the night of the sound bowl class, while I was setting up the recording equipment I told her the entire story, including the "last story" that follows this. It ended with a hug, with an honesty I am happy to have shared and now, for me, the sharing and honesty has also healed our friendship as well. I've just finished a day-long meditation class she led and it was a very positive and uplifting experience, free of any remnants of my desires and illusions.

It wasn't too long after the first part of this story happened that I had the Reiki session that is in "the Last Story."

I'm telling this story now because it was, I guess, the last piece of what I needed to learn and understand to reach what seems to be the end of my grief journey. It filled the last empty places and in the end, I learned that while I had grieved strongly for the loss of the physical part of Andi and my life together, we had learned, fairly early in my grief journey, to allow the spiritual and emotional part of our lives to remain.

Now, with the addition of the affections and the affirmations, all the parts of our lives that I was missing and grieving were no longer absent and so I seem to have been able to let go of my grief because we were still able to share all the parts of our life that I thought were missing.

This is of course only what happened to me and how I interpret it. As I've written a number of times, it isn't meant to be a model for anyone else. It's just my story that I want to tell here both for my own healing and to honor Andi and all we are to each other. It is mostly, though, to put this somewhat different story of a grief journey out there in case anyone is struggling to understand or believe something that looks like what we have found.

So, this seems to have been the last piece for my grief journey. It marks the last thing I needed to learn to reach healing and wellness and to begin to fully live again, to allow love to grow again where pain and sadness and grief used to live within me.

It is, I believe, a hopeful message that in whatever way grief has changed each of us, however we each come to see our lives now, there is always hope for healing and wellness and however it happens to you is just fine. Healing is healing and if you have found a healthy place for yourself where you find peace, acceptance and life, then it is good and it is ok and it is yours.

"The Last Story"... This is the conclusion of the book but it's not really the end of the story...

This story is about something that happened to me after the events in the "Next-to-Last Story," near the end of the fifth year of my grief journey. It was fairly surprising to me when it happened but it is a pretty hopeful sign for possibilities and perhaps an illustration of what an active and forward-looking reconstruction may offer.

Most of the stories I've told here about hope and healing have been about healing. This one is mostly about hope, as it should be.

Of course, as I keep writing, it's just what happened to me and I don't think anyone can or should expect their journeys to look like mine.

At the time this happened, I had been taking yoga classes for a few years with Tammy Black, a very special teacher in my life. Among the many things she taught me and brought into my life was an introduction to Reiki, a way to allow Universal Life Energy and its healing force into one's life.

As part of the process of becoming attuned to Reiki, she did a Reiki alignment session for me one afternoon. After the session, she took some time to tell me about her impressions of the way my body and spirit responded to the energy of Reiki moving through me.

She was already aware of my bereavement before the session and told me that she had expected to feel and find a darkness in my heart were the sadness of bereavement usually resides at that level. So she said she was surprised when instead of darkness in that area, she found light and the image of pink roses growing in my heart. She told me I needed to get a piece of pink (rose) quartz to have in my house, as well. She asked me what I thought it all meant and at first, probably because I was so transported by the Reiki session, it didn't really strike me in any special way.

But when I went home after the session and began to think about it, I realized that it was actually pretty strongly significant. There were lots of connections to my life and to Andi and to my grief journey. First, this book is entitled Flowers from Andrea and the name refers to the flowering "love" plant I've told the story of in Chapter 3.

Second, one of our favorite flowers was the wild pink roses that grow high in the mountains of Rocky Mountain National Park, a place that we loved to visit. Since I'm a geologist, the pink quartz was pretty clear as was the color connection. Third, and I just realized this as I am editing the final version of the book, it is mirrored in the "spiritual gardening" section earlier in this chapter.

But the most interesting connection is that about a month before the Reiki session and after the events in the "next-to-last story," I started to feel a very distinct change in my grieving. I felt a strong change in how I was looking at both the past and the future and a very clear lessening of the sadness and almost all of my other grief emotions.

I even dared to think that maybe I was beginning to not grieve anymore, that I was beginning to live again with all the memories of our life turned to gold and that my past and more amazingly my present and future were appearing without the haze of grief clouding them any longer.

The idea of flowers growing in my heart where my grief used to be kind of filled me with hope and affirmation that all I had done and experienced in my healing journey had allowed me to progress to wellness. It let me begin to believe that I could continue to grow and live and hold our past in a place of honor and have those golden memories in my mind and heart and let go of the grief without feeling any need to experience it any longer.

There are some conflicts here. First, it is almost a given in the bereavement community that you never get over your grief, that you never really stop grieving. So how could I have reached a place where I felt that my grief had ended?

But, could that be a self-fulfilling prophecy? I have to ask myself here, not knowing what the answer is, what is it we are really hoping for during our grief journeys anyway? Isn't it at some level that we will ultimately be healed and have our grief come to an end? If not that, then what else is the final hope in hope and healing about?

Second, through much of my grief journey, there was a feeling of almost guilt that accompanied each new growth in myself, especially when it didn't trigger my grief as I was moving forward in my life, or where I was starting to feel good or happy. So what was this new feeling of being at the end of my grief going to feel like or bring?

So, I'm still working it out. I am still coming to look at the new feelings and emotions and ways of thinking that are developing in me. But the way I feel now has made me very hopeful that maybe my grief has really come to an end but that it in no way diminishes the love or the memories of our life or my continuing connection to Andi in spirit. I just don't have to grieve over it any longer.

Something else I experienced shortly after I had reached this place in my journey was that one day I suddenly realized that something was missing in the way I was feeling. I suddenly realized that I no longer felt any feelings of grief shrouding me. The feeling of a tangible grief cloaking me was gone. And I had never even realized that feeling had been there until it was absent. Hmmm...

And the final piece of this story, as of when I'm writing this, is that on New Years Eve of 2022, Andi and I dedicated ourselves to following a new part of our journey together in spirit. We agreed to sharing yet another chapter in our lives that is us, together in spirit, in love and free of the illness, pain and sadness of her cancer journey and free of the pain and sadness of my grief journey. We are free to build yet more love, in this new way, in the place where the roses are growing in my heart.

And I could now tell the story and write this book!

❀

Hope and Healing… a Conclusion of Sorts:

Finding hope and healing and moving to wellness is never going to be easy. It takes time and effort to learn and grow and make something new out of our often shattered lives. I believe that if we are kind to ourselves, work hard at it and perhaps find others who share our experiences, and we help each other and encourage and support each other, we can make the journey at least a little easier by telling our stories, sharing our grief and knowing that we are not alone, that others are and have been there and survived it too.

This is my hope: that perhaps, maybe with a little help from what we've written here, you will find your way through your own grief journey and in your own way, come to a place of acceptance, wellness and peace so that you can live again, move forward in your live but still honor and treasure all that your love brought you in the part of your lives you shared with your spouse or partner. Our wish for everyone who reads this is for you to find peace and a life full of golden memories of your love and much joy in whatever future you are able to build.

With Hope and Healing from Howard and Andi…

Epilogue

I want to add something here at the end that has happened since I finished writing the last chapter of the book, since I wrote the "last story."

During the past year, my grief journey has clearly come to an end. Though I wrote about uncertainty and wanting to observe how it unfolded in the final chapter, in the months since then, it has become clear to me that I am indeed no longer grieving.

I can say with confidence now that healing and wellness have taken over and I no longer feel any of the feelings of grief that had been a part of my life. The tangible feeling of grief enclosing my body, thoughts and emotions is no longer with me.

While I still may get sad about something from the past, it is just sadness now and not grief. While I still sometimes wish for things we shared in the past, I no longer grieve them. While I sometimes miss the material affection and affirmations our love contained, I no longer grieve because they are absent. I also no longer grieve for the future we didn't get to share.

I appear to have accepted my life and have accepted what it contains and what it doesn't. I am indeed fully living again and the new meaning and purpose I found during my grief journey sustains me and has given me reasons to grow and live in my life as it is.

My experiences over the past year have shown me that it is possible to step beyond grief, to live beyond it and to see it's ending. It is also clear that my memories of my life with Andi remain strong, that nothing of who and what we were has been diminished by the ending of my grief. I am just no longer grieving!

Perhaps it is time passing and the hard work of becoming more that has brought me to this place and this realization, but whatever the reason, I want to end with the very hopeful thought that contrary to expectations, *I am not, and others don't necessarily have to grieve forever.* Our grief may actually come to an end and we may eventually find healing, wellness and life while still remaining full of the love and the memories of the things that made our lives together with our spouses or partners what they were.

In Hope, Healing, Wellness and Life,

Howard,

January, 2023

About the Authors:

Dr. Howard Fischer is a retired Geology Professor who is now mainly a facilitator for support and social groups of bereaved spouses and partners. Howard is the Director and lead Facilitator of Adaire House, providing integrated bereavement support programs for spouses and partners in Northern Colorado. He has just completed a companion to Flowers From Andrea entitled The Adaire House Facilitators Guide... a Guidebook for Support and Discussion Group Meetings for Bereaved Spouses and Partners (available as a digital download at adairehouse.org). Along with his daughter, he owns a CPR training School in Fort Collins, Colorado.

Andrea Adaire Fischer was a multi-talented writer, painter, retailer, and a loving mother and grandmother. She wrote poems and verses and had some of her work published as greeting cards and in anthologies for Blue Mountain Arts. She is now a strong, graceful and beautiful spirit after her eight-year battle with breast cancer came to an end in 2016.

www.ingramcontent.com/pod-product-compliance
Lightning Source LLC
Chambersburg PA
CBHW060016100426
42740CB00010B/1500